DE GUSTIBUS PRESENTS
THE GREAT COOKS' COOKBOOKS

THE ART OF *New American Cooking*

DE GUSTIBUS PRESENTS
THE GREAT COOKS' COOKBOOKS

THE ART OF *New American Cooking*

ARLENE FELTMAN-SAILHAC

PHOTOGRAPHS BY TOM ECKERLE

DESIGN BY MARTIN LUBIN

BLACK DOG & LEVENTHAL

NEW YORK

Published by

Black Dog & Leventhal Publishers, Inc.
151 West 19th Street
New York, NY 10011

Distributed by

Workman Publishing Company
708 Broadway
New York, NY 10003

Manufactured in Hong Kong

ISBN: 1-884822-17-7

h g f e d c b a

Stuffed Cornish Game Hens with Crumb and Sausage Stuffing adapted from *A Family Christmas,* a Reader's Digest Publication. Special thanks to Edwin O. McFarlane at Reed College, Portland, Oregon, for use of this recipe. All of James Beard's recipes used by permission of John Ferrone.

All of Craig Claiborne's recipes adapted from *Craig Claiborne's: A Feast Made for Laughter* by Craig Claiborne. Copyright © 1982 by Craig Claiborne. Used by permission of Doubleday, a division of Bantam Doubleday Dell Publishing Group, Inc., New York.

All of Bradley Ogden's recipes adapted from *Breakfast, Lunch and Dinner* by Bradley Ogden. Copyright © 1991 by Bradley Ogden. Used by permission of Random House, Inc., New York.

Grilled Salmon with Black Pepper and Ginger from *Adventures in the Kitchen* by Wolfgang Puck. Copyright © 1991 by Wolfgang Puck. Adapted by permission of Random House, Inc., New York.

Fresh Tuna with Maui Onions and Avocado, and Pecan Pie from *The Wolfgang Puck Cookbook* by Wolfgang Puck. Copyright © 1986 by Wolfgang Puck. Adapted by permission of Random House, Inc., New York.

Thanks to Anne Rosenzweig for permission to reprint Chocolate Bread Pudding, adapted from *The Arcadia Seasonal Mural and Cookbook* by Anne Rosenzweig. Copyright © 1986 Anne Rosenzweig. Published by Harry N. Abrams, Inc., New York.

Smoked Salmon, Salmon Roe, and Pasta Salad; and Fusilli with Tomatoes and Bread Crumbs, adapted from *Chez Panisse Pasta, Pizza and Calzone* by Alice Waters, Patricia Curtan, and Martine Labro. Copyright © 1984 by Alice Waters, Patricia Curtan, and Martine Labro. Used by permission of Random House, Inc., New York.

Apricot and Cherry Tart adapted from *Chez Panisse Desserts* by Lindsey Remolif Shere. Copyright © 1985 Lindsey Remolif Shere. Used by permission of Random House, Inc., New York.

DEDICATION

I dedicate this book to my family, which loves to eat:

My parents, Adelaide and Stanley Kessler;

My sister, brother-in-law, and niece, Gayle, Stanley, and Amy Miller;

My Grandma Berdie, who opened my eyes to food;

And to Alain Sailhac and Todd Feltman, the two "men in my life who are my favorite dining partners."

ACKNOWLEDGMENTS

During the fourteen-year existence of De Gustibus at Macy's, many people have given their support and encouragement.

First, my profound thanks to all the wonderful chefs and cooks who have taught at De Gustibus at Macy's. A special thanks to David Burke, Craig Claiborne, Michael Lomonaco, Wayne Nish, Bradley Ogden, Charles Palmer, Debra Ponzek, Alfred Portale, Wolfgang Puck, Anne Rosenzweig, Alice Waters, and to the memory of James Beard.

Thanks to my priceless assistants who are always there for me in a million ways: Jane Asche, Barbara Bjorn, Pam Carey, Corinne Gherardi, Yonina Jacobs, Nancy Robbins, and Betti Zucker.

Thanks to Barbara Teplitz for all her help and support throughout the year, and to Gertrud Yampierre for holding the office together.

Thanks to Ruth Schwartz for believing in the concept of De Gustibus and helping to orchestrate its initiation at Macy's.

Thanks to everyone at Macy's Herald Square who has supported De Gustibus at Macy's since its inception, with special notice to the Public Relations and Advertising Departments who helped spread the word.

Thanks to J.P. Leventhal and Pamela Horn of Black Dog & Leventhal Publishers for providing the vehicle to put our cooking classes into book form and for being so encouraging.

A special thanks to Jane Asche for her help during the beginning stages of the book.

Thanks to Tom Eckerle for his magical photographs; Ceci Gallini for her impeccable taste and prop design; and Roscoe Betsill, whose food styling really took this project to another level.

Special thanks for supplying the props to Joe Denofrio at Macy's, N.Y.C.; and to Modern Age, N.Y.C.

Thanks to Marty Lubin for his wonderful design.

Thanks to Mary Goodbody, recipe-testers Deborah Callan and Elizabeth Wheeler, and editors Sarah Bush and Judith Sutton for making the book "user friendly."

Thanks to my agent, Judith Weber, for her help and advice.

Special thanks to Judith Choate, who shaped all my words into meaningful prose and never ceased to amaze me with her knowledge of food and her patience and calm, and to Steve Pool for getting these words into the computer with smiles and enthusiasm.

Heartfelt thanks to the entire Kobrand Corporation, purveyors of fine wine, especially Cathleen Burke and Kimberly Charles for opening the door for the marriage of fine wine and great food for the last ten years.

Finally, thanks to all the faithful De Gustibus customers who have made all our classes spring to life.

Contents

Foreword

Fourteen years ago, the popularity of cooking classes was growing all over the United States. While interest was high, New Yorkers could not always fit an ongoing series of classes into their busy schedules. Demonstration classes seemed to me to be the answer, and De Gustibus was born. What began as four chefs and an electric frying pan on a stage developed into more than 350 chefs and cooking teachers demonstrating their specialties in a professionally equipped kitchen for groups of fervent food-lovers.

When we started De Gustibus in 1980, we had no inkling of the variety of new cuisines that would become an integral part of American cooking. Since then, we have discovered New World Cuisine, Florida Cuisine, Light Cooking, Fusion Cooking, Cajun Cooking, Southwest Cooking-- you name it! As American and international cuisines have changed and our tastes have broadened, De Gustibus has stayed on the cutting edge of the culinary experience. We have invited teachers, cooks, and chefs to De Gustibus both because of their level of renown in the food world, and because of their challenging, unique, current, and, above all, noteworthy cooking styles.

The goal of the cooking demonstrations at De Gustibus is to make the art of the grand master chefs and cooks accessible and practical for the home kitchen. Each chef leads the way and holds out a helping hand to the home cook. The results depend as much on the cook's wit, self-confidence, and interest as they do on a great recipe. Thus, students, and now readers of this book, can learn to master the recipes of the most sophisticated chefs and cooks.

The reason De Gustibus demonstration classes are so popular is that they allow the novice the opportunity to feel the passion--as well as to see each professional chef's or cook's technique, order, and discipline. By seeing how each chef's personality influences the final product, serious home cooks gain the confidence to trust their own tastes and instincts. New and unfamiliar ingredients, untried techniques, and even a little dazzle all find a place in the amateur's kitchen.

This book introduces some of the best and most popular menus demonstrated throughout the years. Each dish is designed to serve six people, unless otherwise noted. All the menus were prepared in class and I have done little to alter them, other than to test and streamline the recipes for the home kitchen. I have also provided each chef's strategy for orchestrating the cooking process, and Kobrand Distributors' wine suggestions for every menu.

ARLENE FELTMAN-SAILHAC
1995

Introduction

The New American chefs' experience at De Gustibus spans some fifteen years. We have, together, participated in the development and recognition of a truly New American cuisine. How exciting it has been to see young chefs in all stages of their careers and to have shared so many momentous occasions with them. Much like being part of a growing family, New American chefs, New American cuisine, and De Gustibus have come up together with all the accompanying feelings of pride in the achievements of each family member.

We have been fortunate to have such illustrious young chefs as Charles Palmer, Debra Ponzek, Alfred Portale, and Anne Rosenzweig begin their teaching careers at De Gustibus, and honored to have culinary icons such as James Beard and Craig Claiborne come on board to inspire us. Each of them has brought new ideas and tastes to the American palate.

Although De Gustibus has featured New American chefs from all over the United States, most of the chefs in this book are from New York City. They have all scaled the heights of their profession and won national recognition from both the press and the public. The representatives from the West Coast have been pioneers in setting the standard for American cooking. All of them serve as models for chefs and home cooks throughout the world.

There is still much debate about what actually constitutes New American cuisine. No matter the outcome of the debate, everyone agrees that the food being cooked in America today is some of the best in the world. This is due in no small part to the chefs in this book. They have insured the availability of high-quality ingredients, often direct from the farmer. They have introduced foods from around the world into our daily fare. They have exercised the flexibility of youth in blending experimentation with tradition. They are all fearless in their determination to bring the best to the American table. As a traditional Italian chef said about a famous American one, "I love to go to his restaurant because he is not steeped in the tradition of his cuisine. He is free to break the rules and come up with

Mise en place tray

something totally innovative, delicious, and exciting that would be against my tradition to try."

All of these non-traditional chefs bring the same discipline to the kitchen as do their classically trained counterparts. As rebellious as our youthful cuisine can be, it still comes to the table backed by order, skill, and taste. In the menus that follow, I believe you will be astonished by the imagination and art of these young lions.

STRATEGIES FOR COOKING FROM OUR CHEFS AND COOKS

Before beginning to prepare any meal, regardless of how simple or complicated, take the following steps to heart:

1 Read through the entire menu and its recipes in advance.

2 Complete ahead of time as many recipes or steps as possible, taking care to allow time for defrosting, reheating, bringing to room temperature, or whatever the recipe requires, before serving.

For each menu we have provided a feature entitled "What You Can Prepare Ahead of Time." This offers time-saving hints for the cook who is preparing the entire menu, or elements of it, and wants to do as much of the preparation as possible before the actual meal. While it is true that many foods taste better fresh rather than reheated, we have included this list for your convenience. These are suggestions, not required do-ahead instructions.

3 Place all the ingredients for a particular recipe on or in individual trays, plates, or bowls, according to the specific steps in the recipe. Each item should be washed, chopped, measured, separated—or whatever is called for—before you begin to cook. This organizational technique, known as the *mise en place* (from the French, it literally means "putting in place"), is the most valuable lesson we at De Gustibus have learned from the pros. We strongly urge you to cook this way.

Note that when a recipe calls for a particular ingredient to be cut in a certain size or shape, it matters. The final result is often dependent upon the textures and colors, as well as the flavors of the ingredients.

4 Use only the best ingredients available. All good chefs and cooks stress this. Try to find the exact ingredient called for, but if you cannot, substitute as suggested in the recipe or glossary, or use your common sense.

5 Rely on your taste buds. They will not lie!

Use the menu suggestions in full, or plan meals around one or two of the elements from a menu. Educate yourself and have fun with the new ingredients and flavors. Now you are ready to join the New American chefs and cooks on a trip through their exciting cuisine.

The Cooks

JAMES BEARD
Late dean of American Cooking, cookbook author, New York, New York

WAYNE NISH
Chef/Owner, *March* and *La Colombe d'Or*, New York, New York

ALFRED PORTALE
Chef/Owner, *Gotham Bar & Grill*, New York, New York

DAVID BURKE
Executive Chef, *Park Avenue Cafe*, New York, New York

BRADLEY OGDEN
Chef/Owner, *Lark Creek Inn*, Larkspur, California

WOLFGANG PUCK
Chef/Owner, *Spago*; *Chinois on Main*, and *Granita*, Los Angeles; *Postrio*, San Francisco, California

CRAIG CLAIBORNE
Cookbook author and former *New York Times* food writer, New York, New York

CHARLES PALMER
Chef/Owner, *Aureole* and *Alva*, New York, New York

ANNE ROSENZWEIG
Chef/Owner, *Arcadia*, New York, New York

MICHAEL LOMONACO
Executive Chef, *'21' Club*, New York, New York

DEBRA PONZEK
Formerly Executive Chef, *Montrachet*, New York, New York

ALICE WATERS
Chef/owner, *Chez Panisse*, Berkeley, California

Techniques

CUTTING VEGETABLES

Into julienne: Using a small, very sharp knife, a mandoline, or an inexpensive vegetable slicer, cut vegetables into thin, uniform sticks, usually about ¼ inch thick and 1 to 2 inches long. This process is easiest when each vegetable is first cut into uniform pieces. For instance, trim a bell pepper into 2 or 3 evenly shaped pieces and then proceed to cut into julienne.

Into dice: Trim vegetables into uniform rectangles. Using a very sharp knife, cut into strips ranging in width from ⅛ to ¼ inch, depending upon the size dice you require. Lay the strips together and cut into even dice by cross-cutting into squares ⅛ to ¼ inch across. When dicing bell peppers, it is particularly important to trim all the membranes and ridges so that you have an absolutely smooth rectangle.

CLARIFYING BUTTER

Clarified butter burns less easily than untreated butter because during the clarifying process, the milk particles are removed. For the same reason, it stores longer.

MAKES ABOUT 3 CUPS

2 pounds unsalted butter, cut into pieces

1 Melt the butter in a medium-sized saucepan over very low heat. Skim off the foam that rises to the top using a ladle, taking care to remove as little of the clear, yellow fat as possible.

2 Let the butter cool slightly and settle. Carefully strain the butter through a fine sieve into a clean, glass container, leaving the milky residue on the bottom of the saucepan. Discard the residue.

3 Cover and refrigerate for up to 2 weeks, or freeze for up to 1 month.

RENDERING DUCK FAT

Place pieces of duck fat in a non-stick sauté pan and cook over very low heat, stirring occasionally, until the fat has melted and all the skin and connective tissue has turned brown and crisp. Remove the "cracklings" from the fat. (Reserve for a salad garnish, if desired.) Strain the fat through a paper coffee filter or a triple layer of cheesecloth to remove any remaining cooked particles. Store, tightly covered and refrigerated, for up to 1 month. Use as you would any animal fat to pan fry potatoes or other foods.

MAKING BREAD CRUMBS

1 SLICE FRESH BREAD YIELDS APPROXIMATELY ½ CUP FRESH BREAD CRUMBS

1 SLICE DRIED (OR TOASTED) BREAD YIELDS APPROXIMATELY ⅓ CUP DRIED BREAD CRUMBS

Trim crusts from slices of firm, homemade-style fresh or dried white bread. Cut the bread into cubes and place in a food processor fitted with the metal blade. Pulse until crumbs are formed.

Store fresh bread crumbs in a tightly covered container in the refrigerator for up to 3 days.

Store dried bread crumbs in a tightly covered container at room temperature for up to 1 month.

TOASTING AND SKINNING NUTS

Preheat oven to 400 degrees F. Lay the nuts in a single layer on a baking sheet or pie tin. Using a spray bottle such as those used to mist plants, lightly spray the nuts with cool water. Roast for 5 to 10 minutes, depending on the nuts' size and oil content, or until golden. Remember, since nuts have a high oil content, they can burn very quickly. Immediately remove from oven and transfer to a cool plate or tray to cool. If you leave them on the baking sheet, they will continue to cook. If the nuts have skins, immediately spread them on a clean kitchen towel. Let them cool slightly and then wrap them in the towel and rub the nuts back and forth to remove the skins.

If you do not need to toast nuts but want to skin them, put them in boiling water for 1 minute. Drain well. Place in a clean kitchen towel and rub the nuts back and forth to remove skins.

Pantry Recipes

Below are standard stock recipes for chicken, duck, and beef, lamb, or veal stock used in the recipes. Homemade stock adds a depth of flavor to a dish not possible with canned broth. However, if time is a factor, use canned chicken (or beef) broth, buying those brands that are labeled "low-sodium." Do not use diluted bouillon cubes; they are excessively salty.

CHICKEN OR DUCK STOCK

MAKES ABOUT 1 QUART
PREPARATION TIME: ABOUT 40 MINUTES
COOKING TIME: ABOUT 2 HOURS AND 30 MINUTES

2 quarts (8 cups) water
2 chicken carcasses or duck carcasses, cut in small pieces
3 onions, chopped
1 carrot, chopped
2 ribs celery, chopped
3 sprigs fresh thyme
3 sprigs fresh parsley
1 bay leaf
1 tablespoon white peppercorns

1 In a large saucepan or stockpot, combine the water and chopped carcasses. Bring to a simmer over medium heat and skim the surface of any foam.

2 Add the onions, carrots, celery, thyme, parsley, bay leaf, and peppercorns. Bring to a boil, reduce the heat, and simmer for 1½ to 2 hours, skimming fat and foam from the surface as necessary, until reduced to 4 cups.

3 Strain the stock through a fine sieve, pressing on the solids to extract as much liquid as possible. Cool to tepid quickly (you can do this by plunging the stockpot into a sinkful of ice). When totally cool, cover, and refrigerate for 6 hours, or until the fat particles have risen to the top. Spoon off the solidified fat and discard.

4 Heat the stock over medium-high heat for about 30 minutes. Adjust the seasonings and use as directed in the specific recipe.

5 To store, cool, then cover and refrigerate for 2 to 3 days or freeze in 1-cup quantities (for ease of use) for up to 3 months.

BEEF, LAMB, OR VEAL STOCK

MAKES ABOUT 3 QUARTS
PREPARATION TIME: ABOUT 40 MINUTES
COOKING TIME: ABOUT 7 HOURS

¼ cup plus 2 tablespoons vegetable oil
4 pounds beef, lamb, or veal marrow bones, chopped into 2-inch pieces
3 onions, peeled and quartered
1 carrot, peeled and chopped
1 rib celery, chopped
1 tomato, quartered
1 bay leaf
1 tablespoon black peppercorns
2 sprigs fresh thyme
3 cloves garlic, crushed
Approximately 4 quarts water

1 Preheat the oven to 450 degrees F.

2 Using ¼ cup of the oil, lightly oil the bones. Spread the bones in a single layer in a large roasting pan. Roast the bones, turning occasionally, for 20 minutes, or until bones are dark golden brown on all sides.

3 Transfer the bones to a large saucepan or stockpot. Add the remaining 2 tablespoons of the oil to roasting pan and stir in the onions, carrot, celery, and tomato. Cook on top of the stove for about 15 minutes over medium-high heat until brown, stirring frequently.

4 With a slotted spoon, transfer the vegetables to the stockpot. Add the bay leaf, peppercorns, thyme, and garlic.

5 Pour off the fat from the roasting pan and discard. Set the pan over moderate heat and deglaze it with 2 cups water, scraping up any particles sticking to the bottom. Add this liquid to the stockpot. Pour enough of the remaining water into the stockpot to cover the bones by 2 inches and bring to a boil. Reduce the heat and let the stock barely simmer, uncovered, for 6 hours, skimming fat and foam from the surface as necessary. Cool, cover and refrigerate for 12 hours or overnight.

6 Strain the stock through a sieve into a clean pan. Discard the solids. Spoon off any trace of fat. Place stockpot over high heat and bring stock to a rolling boil. Lower heat and simmer for 30 minutes, or until the flavor is full-bodied and the stock has reduced slightly. Adjust seasonings and use as directed in the specific recipe.

7 To store, cool quickly (you can do this by plunging stockpot into a sinkful of ice). When totally cool, cover, and refrigerate for 2 to 3 days or freeze in 1-cup quantities (for ease of use) for up to 3 months.

FISH STOCK

MAKES ABOUT 3 CUPS

PREPARATION TIME: ABOUT 20 MINUTES

COOKING TIME: ABOUT 35 MINUTES

Making fish stock is easier and faster than making chicken or beef stock. Substituting a canned broth is tricky in recipes calling for fish stock; but if you have no time to make stock, substitute low-sodium canned chicken broth for fish stock.

2 sprigs fresh parsley
2 sprigs fresh thyme
1 small bay leaf
2 pounds fish bones (from saltwater fish such as sole, John Dory, turbot, halibut, or other very fresh, non-oily fish), chopped into pieces
2 tablespoons canola or other flavorless oil
1 small onion, chopped
1 small rib celery, chopped
1 cup dry white wine

1 Make a *bouquet garni* by tying the parsley, thyme, and bay leaf together with kitchen twine. Set aside.

2 Clean the fish bones under cold running water, removing the gills from the heads and any traces of blood.

3 Heat the oil in a large saucepan or stockpot over medium heat. Add the fish bones and vegetables. Lower the heat and lay a piece of wax paper directly on the ingredients in the pan. Cook for 10 minutes, stirring once or twice to prevent browning. (Be careful not to push the paper into the pan.)

4 Remove the wax paper. Add the wine and enough water to cover the bones and vegetables by 2 inches. Add the *bouquet garni*. Increase the heat to high, bring to a boil, and skim the surface of all foam. Lower the heat and simmer for 20 to 25 minutes.

5 Strain the stock through an extra-fine sieve. Discard the solids. Use as directed in the specific recipe.

6 To store, cool quickly (you can do this by plunging the stockpot into a sinkful of ice). When totally cool, cover tightly, and refrigerate for 2 to 3 days or freeze in 1-cup quantities (for ease of use) for up to 3 weeks.

VEGETABLE STOCK

MAKES ABOUT 3 CUPS

PREPARATION TIME: ABOUT 20 MINUTES

COOKING TIME: ABOUT 2 HOURS

Making vegetable stock is easy and fast. Substituting a canned broth is difficult, as finding a good one can be a problem. Low-sodium vegetable bouillon cubes, sold in health food stores, are a good substitute. Low-sodium canned chicken broth can also be used in recipes calling for vegetable stock.

3 quarts cold water
1 carrot, peeled and chopped
1 potato, peeled and chopped
1 large onion, chopped
3 ribs celery, chopped
1/2 leek, white part only, chopped
1 small tomato, chopped
1 tablespoon salt, or to taste
2 cloves garlic, peeled
1 teaspoon chopped fresh parsley
1/2 teaspoon black peppercorns

1 In a large saucepan, bring 1 cup of the water to a boil over medium-high heat. Add the carrot, potato, onions, celery, leeks, tomatoes, and salt. Cook for 5 minutes, stirring occasionally.

2 Add the remaining 11 cups water to the pan, along with the garlic, parsley, and peppercorns. Bring to a simmer, reduce the heat to low, and simmer gently for 2 hours.

3 Strain the stock through a fine sieve into a bowl. Discard the vegetables. Let cool for 1 hour, and then pour the stock through a fine sieve again. Use as directed in the specific recipe.

4 To store, cool, cover, and refrigerate for up to 3 days or freeze in 1-cup quantities (for ease of use) for up to 3 months.

COOKED BEANS

MAKES ABOUT 2 ½ CUPS COOKED BEANS
PREPARATION TIME: ABOUT 10 MINUTES
COOKING TIME: 1 TO 2 HOURS
SOAKING TIME: AT LEAST 4 HOURS

Cooking dried beans is simply a matter of reconstituting them by soaking and long, slow cooking. You can double or triple the basic recipe. Cooked beans keep in the freezer for up to 1 month and in the refrigerator for four or five days. Lentils and black-eyed peas do not require soaking before cooking.

1 cup black, white, fava or other dried bean

1 Check the beans for pebbles and other debris. Rinse them well in a colander. Put the beans in a large pot and add about 10 cups of water (10 times the amount of beans). Cover and let soak at room temperature for at least 4 hours. Change the water 3 times during soaking. If the beans are particularly old, let them soak for 8 hours or overnight.

2 Drain the beans, rinse with cold water, and return to the pot. Add fresh, cold water to cover the beans by about 2 inches. Bring to a boil over high heat, skim the foam that rises to the surface, and reduce the heat to a simmer. Cover and cook for 1 to 2 hours until tender, adding more water to the pot as necessary. The beans are done when they are fork-tender. Drain and proceed with the specific recipe.

Note: To prepare beans by the "quick-soak method," put the beans in a large pot and add enough water to cover by 3 inches. Bring to a boil and boil for 5 minutes. Remove from the heat, cover, and soak for no less than 1 hour and no longer than 2 hours. Drain and rinse well. This eliminates the long soaking. Proceed with the cooking instructions above.

A THANKSGIVING ALTERNATIVE

*Cornish Game Hens with
Crumb and Sausage Stuffing*

Beet and Carrot Puree

Quince Tart

WINE SUGGESTIONS:

Pinot Noir *(main course)*
Late Harvest Riesling *(dessert)*

WHAT YOU CAN PREPARE AHEAD OF TIME

Up to 3 days ahead: Make the Beet and Carrot Puree. Cover and refrigerate. Reheat as directed.

The day before: Make the Quince Tart. Cover loosely and store in a cool area of the kitchen.

Early in the day: Make the Crumb and Sausage Stuffing for the hens. Cover and refrigerate. Do not stuff the hens until ready to roast.

Having James Beard teach at De Gustibus was a complete culinary experience. It was like having the father of all fathers cooking in our presence, talking about our favorite subject, and his: food. Mr. Beard made his love and understanding of American ingredients come alive at our stove. He reminisced about the quince trees growing in the yard of his boyhood home and told of his excitement at discovering the old-fashioned quince tart that we include here, on the menu of the award-winning Coach House restaurant in New York City.

James Beard prepared this menu for a small gathering at Thanksgiving, but he felt it would also make a warming fall dinner. Although this class came late in the career of this giant of American cuisine, it was an afternoon we will never forget. James Beard truly paved the way for New American cooking.

◁ JAMES BEARD: Quince Tart (recipe on page 20)

Cornish Game Hens with Crumb and Sausage Stuffing

SERVES 6
PREPARATION TIME: ABOUT 15 MINUTES
COOKING TIME: ABOUT 1 HOUR AND 30 MINUTES

Individual game hens are a great alternative to the mammoth holiday turkey. They require a shorter cooking time and particularly appeal to those who want both white and dark meat.

6 Rock Cornish game hens (about 1 pound each), rinsed and patted dry
½ cup unsalted butter
¼ cup sliced scallions
8 ounces bulk sausage meat
1 tablespoon chopped fresh tarragon
2 teaspoons salt, or to taste
1 teaspoon freshly ground black pepper, or to taste
4 cups fresh bread crumbs (see page 12)
¼ cup chopped fresh parsley

1 Preheat the oven to 400 degrees F. Assemble the *mise en place* trays for this recipe (see page 9).

2 In a large sauté pan, melt the butter over medium-high heat. Add the scallions and sauté for 4 minutes, or until just limp. Stir in the sausage meat, tarragon, salt, and pepper. Cook for 8 to 10 minutes, or until the sausage begins to lose its pinkness. Add the bread crumbs and parsley and stir until well combined. Remove from the heat and let cool completely.

3 Place an equal portion of the stuffing into each of the hens. Truss the cavities closed (see page 93) by sewing with kitchen twine, or secure them with skewers.

4 Place the stuffed hens on a rack in a large roasting pan, breast side up. Roast for 15 minutes. Turn hens over and baste for another 15 minutes with the accumulated juices.

5 Reduce the oven temperature to 350 degrees F. Turn the birds breast side up, baste again, and roast for about 45 minutes longer, or until just tender; do not overcook.

6 Remove the pan from oven and allow the hens to rest for 5 minutes before serving. Spoon the pan juices over the hens and serve on warm dinner plates.

▶ **To test the hens for doneness, wiggle the legs and pierce the joint between the body and thigh with a sharp knife. If legs move freely and the juices run clear, the birds are ready.**

▶ **Do not stuff the birds until just before cooking. Harmful bacteria may develop in the stuffing as it sits in the uncooked bird.**

▷ JAMES BEARD: Cornish Game Hens with Crumb and Sausage Stuffing; Beet and Carrot Puree

Beet and Carrot Puree

SERVES 6
PREPARATION TIME: ABOUT 20 MINUTES
COOKING TIME: ABOUT 1 HOUR AND 15 MINUTES

The beautiful color of this vegetable puree simply sings "fall." It can be prepared well ahead of time, which makes it a perfect holiday side dish.

1 pound young beets, trimmed and scrubbed
1 tablespoon vegetable oil
1 pound carrots, peeled, trimmed, and thinly sliced
4 tablespoons unsalted butter, at room temperature
1/8 teaspoon freshly grated nutmeg
Salt and freshly ground black pepper to taste

1 Preheat the oven to 300 degrees F. Assemble the *mise en place* trays for this recipe (see page 9).

2 Rub the beets with the oil and wrap in aluminum foil. Place on a baking sheet and bake for 1 hour, or until the beets are tender when pierced with a fork. Let cool slightly.

3 Meanwhile, place the carrots in a medium-sized saucepan and add enough water to cover. Bring to a boil over high heat. Lower the heat and simmer, covered, for about 15 minutes, or until tender. Drain well and set aside.

4 Peel the beets and discard the skins. Cut the beets into quarters.

5 Put the beets, carrots, butter, and nutmeg in a food processor fitted with the metal blade, and process until smooth. Season to taste with salt and pepper.

6 Transfer the puree to a medium-sized saucepan. Cook over medium heat, stirring constantly, for about 3 minutes, or until just heated through. Serve hot.

▶ Reserve the trimmed beet greens to use as a salad vegetable, or steam for a delicious and nutritious green vegetable.

Quince Tart

SERVES 6
PREPARATION TIME: ABOUT 45 MINUTES
COOKING AND BAKING TIME: ABOUT 2 HOURS AND 10 MINUTES
CHILLING TIME (PASTRY ONLY): AT LEAST 1 HOUR
COOLING TIME (TART): ABOUT 3 HOURS

This tart is an old-fashioned American autumn dessert. Although quinces are usually available only from October through December, they can be wrapped in plastic and refrigerated for up to two months.

FILLING:

6 large quinces
1 cinnamon stick
2 whole cloves
3 cups water
3 cups granulated sugar
Juice of 1 lemon

PASTRY:

2 1/2 cups all-purpose flour
1 cup unsalted butter, cut into small pieces and softened
2 tablespoons granulated sugar

3 large egg yolks
1/2 teaspoon ground cinnamon
Grated zest of 1 lemon

GARNISH:

2 tablespoons chopped, toasted almonds
1 cup heavy cream, gently whipped to soft peaks

■ Special Equipment: 12-inch fluted tart pan with removable bottom; pie weights; pastry cutter (optional).

1 Assemble the *mise en place* trays for this recipe (see page 9).

2 To make the filling, peel and core the quinces, reserving the seeds. Cut the quinces into julienne strips and set aside.

3 Wrap the cinnamon stick, cloves, and quince seeds in a cheesecloth bag and tie securely.

20

4 In a large, heavy-bottomed saucepan, combine the water, sugar, and lemon juice. Bring to a boil over high heat. Stir in the julienned quinces and the spice bag and return the liquid to a boil. Reduce the heat and simmer, stirring occasionally, for about 1½ hours, or until the quinces are very soft and the mixture has thickened. Remove the pan from the heat and discard the spice bag. Set aside to cool.

5 Meanwhile, to make the pastry, put the flour in a medium-sized bowl and make a well in the center. Add the butter, 2 tablespoons of the sugar, the egg yolks, ground cinnamon, and lemon zest. Using your fingertips, knead to form dough. Gather into a ball and divide into two pieces, one about a third larger than the other. Flatten each into a disk, wrap in plastic, and refrigerate for at least 1 hour, or until firm.

6 Preheat the oven to 375 degrees F.

7 Roll out two thirds of the pastry between 2 pieces of wax paper, or on a lightly floured board, to a circle about 14 inches in diameter. Carefully fit into a 12-inch fluted tart pan with a removable bottom. Trim the edges. Prick the bottom of the tart with a fork, line it with foil, and weight with pie weights, rice, or beans.

8 Bake the tart shell for 10 minutes. Remove the foil and weights and fill with the cooled quince mixture.

9 Roll out the remaining third of pastry to a 12-inch circle. Using a pastry cutter or a knife, cut into strips ¼ inch to ½ inch wide. Using the longest strips for the center of the tart and, working from the center out, lay half of the strips about ¾ inch apart across the tart. Lay the remaining strips perpendicular to the first strips to form a lattice. Trim off the excess dough and push the ends of the strips into the edge of the crust to seal.

10 Bake the tart for 20 to 30 minutes, or until the pastry is golden brown and the filling is bubbling. Remove from the oven and sprinkle with the almonds. Cool on a wire rack for at least 3 hours, or overnight. Do not refrigerate.

11 Serve at room temperature, with whipped cream.

▶ **The pectin in the quince seeds acts as a thickening agent for the tart filling.**

▶ **The tart is also good served with crème fraîche, sour cream, or vanilla ice cream instead of whipped cream.**

A WELCOME-TO-SPRING DINNER

*Red Potato and Goat Cheese Tart
with Frisée and Bacon Salad*

*Spice-Crusted Tuna with Asparagus
and Seaweed-Wrapped Noodles*

*Orange and Strawberry Tart
with Candied Bell Pepper Caramel*

WINE SUGGESTIONS:

Sauvignon Blanc *(first and second course)*
Vin Santo *(dessert)*

WHAT YOU CAN PREPARE AHEAD OF TIME

Up to 1 week ahead: Make the Basil and Curry Oils. Store in a tightly covered, glass or ceramic container in the refrigerator. Bring to room temperature before using. Grind the spices for the Spice-Crusted Tuna. Store in an airtight container at room temperature.

The day before: Make the Basil Oil for the Red Potato and Goat Cheese Tart, if not already made. Store in a tightly covered, glass container in a cool, dark place.

Early in the day: Make the nori rolls for the Spice-Crusted Tuna. Cover and refrigerate. Bring to room temperature before serving. Cook the asparagus for the Spice-Crusted Tuna. Cover and refrigerate. Bring to room temperature before serving. Clean the greens for the Red Potato and Goat Cheese Tart. Dry and refrigerate until ready to use. Bake the pastry for the Orange and Strawberry Tart. Prepare the fruit for the Orange and Strawberry Tart. Cover and refrigerate. Make the Candied Bell Pepper Caramel. Cover and refrigerate until needed. Just before serving, reheat gently.

Up to 1 hour before the party: Assemble the Red Potato and Goat Cheese Tart. Make the warm vinaigrette for the Frisée and Bacon Salad. Strain the Basil Oil.

D avid Burke is truly one of the most imaginative chefs to have taught at De Gustibus. He tells us that he has been inspired to create his fantasy recipes by observing the commonplace or by watching something as ordinary as a McDonald's television commercial. Obviously, David's food knows no boundaries. His inspiration seems to come from all cuisines, cultures, and lifestyles, as he creates dishes that are always beyond anyone's expectations. This menu showcases ingredients that are at their tastiest during the spring months and includes hints of the flavors of France, Asia, and the American Southwest.

◁ DAVID BURKE: Orange and Strawberry Tart with Candied Bell Pepper Caramel
(recipe on page 28)

Red Potato and Goat Cheese Tart with Frisée and Bacon Salad

SERVES 6
PREPARATION TIME: ABOUT 1 HOUR AND 10 MINUTES
COOKING TIME: ABOUT 1 HOUR
RESTING TIME (BASIL OIL ONLY): AT LEAST 24 HOURS

Many flavors are magnificently combined to make these tasty tarts. Hints of the flavors of Mexico, the Middle East, and France are pulled together in a totally American fashion.

10 medium Red Bliss potatoes, washed and dried
1/2 cup plus 2 tablespoons olive oil
2 tablespoons ground cumin
1 teaspoon chopped fresh rosemary
Kosher salt and freshly ground black pepper to taste
12 strips bacon, diced
1/2 pound semisoft goat cheese
6 store-bought flour tortillas
1/2 cup chopped fresh chives
6 tablespoons mustard oil (see note)
3 tablespoons tarragon vinegar
1 large head frisée, trimmed, rinsed, and dried
1 cup baby spinach leaves, trimmed, rinsed, and dried
Goat Cheese Fondue (recipe follows)
1/2 cup olivada (see note)
1/2 cup cored, peeled, seeded, and diced tomatoes
3 tablespoons Basil Oil (recipe follows)

1 Preheat the oven to 350 degrees F. Assemble the *mise en place* trays for this recipe (see page 9).

2 In a shallow roasting pan, combine the potatoes with 1/4 cup of the olive oil, the cumin, rosemary, and salt and pepper to taste, and toss to coat. Roast for about 30 minutes, or until the potatoes are tender when pierced with a fork. Set aside to cool.

3 Meanwhile, in a medium-sized sauté pan, cook the diced bacon over medium-low heat for 6 to 8 minutes, or until crisp. Lift the bacon from the pan with a slotted spoon and drain on paper towels. Pour off all but 3 tablespoons of the bacon fat, and set the pan aside to use for the vinaigrette.

4 In a small bowl, combine the goat cheese with 2 tablespoons of the olive oil and salt and pepper to taste. Beat with a wooden spoon until smooth.

5 Cut the tortillas into 4 1/2-inch rounds. Generously coat each one with the goat cheese mixture.

6 Slice the cooked potatoes crosswise into thin slices. Arrange them overlapping slightly, around the edges of the tortillas. Sprinkle with the chives, and season to taste with salt and pepper. Set aside.

7 Set the pan with the bacon fat over low heat. Stir in the mustard oil and vinegar. Cook, stirring, for about 1 minute, or until the vinaigrette is well blended and warm. Remove from the heat and cover to keep warm.

8 Divide the remaining 1/4 cup olive oil between 2 large skillets and heat over medium-high heat. When the oil is hot, lay 3 tortilla tarts, potato side down, in each pan. Cook for 3 minutes, or until the potatoes are crisp. Carefully turn and cook for 1 additional minute longer, or until the tortillas are crisp. Remove from the skillets and drain on paper towels.

9 In a large bowl, combine the frisée and spinach with the cooked bacon. Pour the warm vinaigrette over the top, and toss to coat. Arrange the salad on 6 plates. Lay the warm tarts on top and spoon some Goat Cheese Fondue, olivada, and diced tomatoes on top of the tarts. Drizzle with Basil Oil. Serve immediately.

NOTE: Mustard oil and olivada (black olive puree) are available from specialty food stores. Mustard oil is also sold in Asian markets, and olivada in good Italian delicatessens. Both can be used as pungent accents in salads, stir fries, sauces, and dressings.

▶ **Make sure the oil is good and hot before cooking.**

◁ DAVID BURKE: Red Potato and Goat Cheese Tart with Frisée and Bacon Salad

GOAT CHEESE FONDUE
MAKES ABOUT 1 CUP

1 teaspoon unsalted butter
2 shallots, minced
3 ounces semisoft goat cheese
1/2 cup light cream
1/2 teaspoon ground cumin
Salt and freshly ground black pepper to taste

1 In a small sauté pan, melt the butter over medium heat. Add the shallots and sauté for about 2 minutes until just softened.

2 Stir in the cheese and cream. Increase the heat to medium-high and cook, stirring constantly for about 1 minute, or until the cheese has melted. Stir in the cumin and salt and pepper to taste. Remove from the heat and keep warm.

BASIL OIL
MAKES ABOUT 3 CUPS

2 bunches fresh basil, leaves only
2 1/2 cups extra-virgin olive oil

1 Dip the basil into a pot of rapidly boiling salted water for 30 seconds. Immediately place into a bowl of lightly salted ice water. Drain and squeeze to remove all the water.

2 In a blender, combine the basil and 1/2 cup of the olive oil. With the blender running, slowly add the remaining 2 cups of oil. Pour the mixture into a non-reactive container. Cover and let rest for 24 hours.

3 Strain the oil through a double layer of cheesecloth or fine strainer into a glass or ceramic bowl. Use right away or cover and refrigerate for up to 1 month. Let come to room temperature before using.

Spice-Crusted Tuna with Asparagus and Seaweed-Wrapped Noodles

SERVES 6
PREPARATION TIME: ABOUT 1 HOUR AND 15 MINUTES
COOKING TIME: ABOUT 30 MINUTES

Again, flavors from all over the world unite to make a contemporary American dish. This is as visually appealing as it is delicious. One of the benefits of this recipe is that the Seaweed-Wrapped Noodle rolls can be made separately and served as an hors d'oeuvre with the yogurt and curry mixture as a dipping sauce.

1/4 cup black peppercorns
1/4 cup fennel seeds
1/4 cup coriander seeds
3/4 tablespoon allspice berries
1/4 cup curry powder
3/4 tablespoon coarse salt
18 thin asparagus spears, approximately the same diameter, trimmed
4 ounces soba noodles
2 tablespoons tahini paste
1/2 cup soy sauce
1 tablespoon rice wine vinegar
3 1/2 tablespoons chopped fresh cilantro
Cayenne pepper to taste

6 sheets nori
3/4 cup plain yogurt
1/2 cup Dijon mustard
6 four-ounce fresh tuna steaks
1/4 cup Curry Oil (recipe follows)

1 Assemble the *mise en place* trays for this recipe (see page 9).

2 Combine the peppercorns, fennel seeds, coriander seeds, and allspice berries in a spice or coffee grinder or a mini food processor and process until very fine. Transfer to a shallow bowl and stir in the curry powder and salt. Set aside.

3 Place the asparagus spears on a steamer rack. Steam for 2 to 3 minutes or until crisp-tender. Pat dry and set aside.

4 Cook the soba noodles in boiling, salted water according to the package directions. Drain well (do not rinse).

▷ DAVID BURKE: Spice-Crusted Tuna with Asparagus and Seaweed-Wrapped Noodles

26

5 In a medium-sized bowl, combine the noodles, tahini, 1/4 cup of the soy sauce, vinegar, 1 1/2 tablespoons of the cilantro, and cayenne to taste.

6 Generously brush the nori sheets with the remaining soy sauce. Place equal portions of the noodle mixture about 1 inch from the bottom edge of each nori sheet. Fold the bottom edge of each sheet over the filling and roll up to make a firm log. Set aside.

7 In a small bowl, combine the yogurt, mustard, and the remaining 3 tablespoons cilantro. Set aside.

8 Dredge the tuna steaks with the spice mixture, pressing it gently into the flesh.

9 In a large sauté pan, heat 3 tablespoons of the Curry Oil over medium-high heat. When the oil is very hot, add the tuna steaks. Sear for 30 seconds per side. Remove from the heat and drain on paper towels.

10 Using a small sharp knife, pierce 3 holes into the side of each steak. Gently push an asparagus spear into each hole, pushing the asparagus as far into the steak as possible. Trim off any excess asparagus so that none extends from the side of the steak.

11 Thinly slice each tuna steak and arrange on 6 serving plates. You will be able to see the asparagus in each slice. Slice each nori noodle roll crosswise on the diagonal. Arrange the nori rolls beside the tuna. Drizzle the plate with the yogurt mixture and the remaining 1 tablespoon Curry Oil.

CURRY OIL
MAKES ABOUT 2 CUPS

2 cups olive oil
1 shallot, minced
1 1/2 tablespoons curry powder
1 teaspoon fennel seeds
1 teaspoon pink peppercorns
Kosher salt and freshly ground pepper to taste

1 In a medium-sized heavy saucepan, heat 1/4 cup of the oil over very low heat. Add the shallot, curry powder, fennel seeds, peppercorns, and salt and pepper to taste. Sauté, stirring constantly, for 2 minutes to allow the curry flavor to develop.

2 Add the remaining oil and simmer gently for about 10 minutes. Remove the pan from the heat and set aside until the solids have settled to the bottom of the pan.

3 Carefully pour the oil into a squeeze bottle or glass jar, leaving the sediment in the pan. Store the oil, tightly covered, in the refrigerator for up to 1 month. Let it come to room temperature before using.

▶ **Serve Curry Oil with grilled fish, lamb, chicken, or on falafel. Stir into rice in place of butter. Sauté fish or chicken cutlets or stir-fry vegetables in it. Drizzle a few drops of oil on cream soups before serving.**

Orange and Strawberry Tart with Candied Bell Pepper Caramel

SERVES 6
PREPARATION TIME: ABOUT 1 HOUR
BAKING AND COOKING TIME: ABOUT 50 MINUTES
CHILLING TIME (PASTRY ONLY): 40 MINUTES

David Burke loves to shock the palate by using foods in interesting ways—for example, bell peppers in a dessert sauce.

PASTRY:

One 10-inch sheet frozen puff pastry
1 teaspoon ground cinnamon
2 tablespoons granulated sugar
2 tablespoons dark brown sugar

FILLING:

2 pints medium strawberries, rinsed, dried, and hulled
4 oranges
Candied Bell Pepper Caramel (recipe follows)
1 cup heavy cream, gently whipped to soft peaks
Mint sprigs

1 Assemble the *mise en place* trays for this recipe (see page 9).

2 Let the puff pastry thaw at room temperature for about 20 minutes. Roll out the puff pastry between two sheets of wax paper to about 1/8 inch thick. Lay on a baking sheet, cover with wax paper, and refrigerate for 30 minutes.

3 Meanwhile, in a small bowl, combine the granulated sugar, brown sugar, and cinnamon. Set aside.

4 To make the filling, remove the zest from the oranges and put in a bowl. Be sure to peel only the colorful zest—not the bitter white pith.

5 Holding each one over the bowl with the zest, peel the oranges and cut between the membranes to separate into sections. Let the sections and any juice fall into the bowl. Discard the membrane and seeds. Set aside.

6 Preheat the oven to 350 degrees F.

7 Remove the pastry from the refrigerator. Place on a board and invert a 10-inch plate over the pastry. With a pastry cutter or sharp knife, cut around the plate to make a 10-inch circle. Carefully transfer the pastry to a nonstick baking sheet, lifting it gently or using spatulas to guide it. Using the point of a sharp knife, prick holes in a circular pattern over the entire surface of the pastry. Refrigerate for 10 minutes.

8 Sprinkle half the sugar mixture over the pastry circle. Bake for about 10 minutes or until the pastry is golden brown. Remove the pastry but do not turn off the oven.

9 Using a spatula, carefully slide the baked crust onto a flat plate. Lay the baking sheet over the plate and invert the pastry onto it, so that the bottom is facing up. Sprinkle the pastry with the remaining sugar mixture. Bake for 5 to 7 minutes longer, or until golden brown.

10 Allow the pastry to cool for 5 minutes and then carefully slide it onto a cake platter.

11 Warm the Candied Bell Pepper Caramel in a small nonreactive saucepan over low heat.

12 Spread the whipped cream over the pastry. Arrange the strawberries, points up, in 2 rows around the edge of the pastry. Mound the orange sections, zest, and juices in a heap in the center of the pastry so that the casual look of the oranges contrasts with the neat rows of strawberries. Pour the warm Candied Bell Pepper Caramel over the fruit. Garnish with mint sprigs and serve immediately.

▶ **If you have extra strawberries, slice them and mix in with the orange sections before mounding them on the cream.**

CANDIED BELL PEPPER CARAMEL
MAKES ABOUT 3 1/2 CUPS

3/4 cup minced yellow bell pepper
3/4 cup minced red bell pepper
1 cup granulated sugar
1 cup apple cider
1 to 2 tablespoons Grand Marnier
3 tablespoons unsalted butter, at room temperature

1 In a medium-sized, heavy, nonreactive saucepan, combine the peppers, sugar, and cider. Cook, stirring occasionally, for about 30 minutes, or until the sauce turns golden brown, thickens, and caramelizes.

2 Remove from the heat and whisk in the Grand Marnier and butter. Cover and refrigerate. Reheat gently before using.

A TOTALLY '50S LUNCH

*Janice Okun's Buffalo Chicken Wings
with Blue Cheese Dressing*

Mrs. Reardy's Shrimp and Artichoke Casserole

Hazelnut Cheesecake

WINE SUGGESTIONS:

Beer or Chardonnay

WHAT YOU CAN PREPARE AHEAD OF TIME

Up to 2 days ahead: Make the Blue Cheese Dressing for the Buffalo Chicken Wings.

Early in the day: Prepare the chicken wings for frying. Wrap tightly and refrigerate. Deep-fry just before serving. Prepare the components of the Shrimp and Artichoke Casserole. Cover and refrigerate the shrimp, mushroom-cream sauce, and the artichokes separately. Assemble the casserole just before baking. Bake the Cheesecake.

Craig Claiborne's lunch will take you back in time to roller skates, hula hoops, saddle shoes, and Junior League cookbooks. This menu could be the centerpiece of a nostalgia party, as you transport your guests to another time and place.

Having Craig Claiborne teach at De Gustibus was truly a memorable experience. We had all read his *New York Times* column, his newspaper and magazine articles, and used his cookbooks with great frequency. In some ways, it seemed as though we were old friends. To have such a culinary personage in our kitchen was thrilling.

Mr. Claiborne is a cook who believes in exactitude. In preparation for his class, we had carefully measured all the ingredients, but he insisted on remeasuring and reweighing everything. Having written thousands of recipes for the home cook, he sent us a clear message: "You can never be too careful when you are writing for the public."

◁ Craig Claiborne: Mrs. Reardy's Shrimp and Artichoke Casserole (recipe on page 33)

Janice Okun's Buffalo Chicken Wings with Blue Cheese Dressing

SERVES 6
PREPARATION TIME: ABOUT 25 MINUTES
COOKING TIME: ABOUT 35 MINUTES

Here's a great recipe for one of America's all-time favorite bar foods. Craig Claiborne brings chicken wings into the dining room as an appetizer, but you could easily increase the amount for a big bowl of tasty party fare.

BLUE CHEESE DRESSING:

1 cup mayonnaise

1/2 cup sour cream

1/4 cup crumbled blue cheese

2 tablespoons minced onion

1 teaspoon minced parsley

1 tablespoon fresh lemon juice

1 tablespoon white vinegar

Salt and freshly ground black pepper to taste

Cayenne pepper to taste

CHICKEN WINGS:

4 pounds chicken wings

Salt and freshly ground black pepper to taste

About 4 cups peanut, vegetable, or corn oil, for deep-frying

4 tablespoons salted butter

2 tablespoons hot red pepper sauce

1 tablespoon white vinegar

24 to 30 four-inch celery sticks

1 Preheat the oven to 250 degrees F. Assemble the *mise en place* trays for this recipe (see page 9).

2 To make the dressing, combine the mayonnaise, sour cream, blue cheese, onion, parsley, lemon juice, and vinegar in a bowl. Add salt, pepper, and cayenne to taste. Cover and refrigerate for at least 1 hour.

3 To prepare the chicken, wash the wings and dry well. Cut off and discard the small tip of each wing. Cut apart the wings at the joint. Sprinkle with salt and pepper to taste.

4 In a deep-fat fryer or a large, deep saucepan, heat the oil over medium-high heat until almost smoking. Add half of the wings and cook for about 10 minutes, stirring occasionally or turning with tongs, until golden brown and crisp. Drain well on paper towels or a brown paper bag. Put the drained wings on a baking sheet and keep warm in the oven while you cook the remaining wings. Drain well and place on the baking sheet in the oven.

CRAIG CLAIBORNE: Janice Okun's Buffalo Chicken Wings with Blue Cheese Dressing

5 In a small saucepan, melt the butter over low heat. Stir in the hot sauce and vinegar.

6 Put the chicken wings on a warm serving platter and pour the butter mixture over them. Serve with the Blue Cheese Dressing and celery sticks.

▶ If you wish to avoid some of the fat in this dish, prepare the recipe through step 3, then in a non-stick baking dish, bake the wings in the oven at 400 degrees F. for about 25 to 30 minutes, or until the wings are brown and crisp. Continue as directed preparing the sauce and serving.

Mrs. Reardy's Shrimp and Artichoke Casserole

Ah, for the days of cholesterol, fat, and calorie ignorance! I suspect that you could replace the butter with canola oil, the milk and cream with skim milk. But I also suspect the result would be less than rich and delicious. Save this recipe for a day when calories don't count and enjoy yourself!

7 tablespoons unsalted butter
1 pound medium shrimp (unshelled)
4½ tablespoons all-purpose flour
¾ cup milk
¾ cup heavy cream
Salt and freshly ground black pepper to taste
4 ounces fresh mushrooms, sliced (about 1¼ cups)
1 nine-ounce package frozen artichoke hearts, thawed and well drained
2 tablespoons sherry
1 tablespoon Worcestershire sauce
¼ cup freshly grated Parmesan cheese
Paprika

1 Preheat the oven to 375 degrees F. Assemble the *mise en place* trays for this recipe (see page 9). Grease a 2-quart casserole or baking dish with 1 tablespoon of the butter.

2 In a pan of rapidly boiling salted water, cook the shrimp for 3 minutes or until just opaque. Drain and refresh under cold running water. Peel and devein. Set aside.

3 In a medium-sized saucepan, melt 4½ tablespoons of the butter over medium-high heat. Whisk in the flour until blended. Gradually whisk in the milk and cream, and cook, whisking constantly, for 3 to 4 minutes, until the sauce is thick and smooth. Season to taste with salt and pepper. Remove from the heat and set aside.

4 In a small sauté pan, melt the remaining 1½ tablespoons butter over medium heat. Add the mushrooms and sauté for about 5 minutes, or until softened. Remove from the heat.

5 Arrange the artichokes in the bottom of the prepared casserole. Scatter the shrimp over the artichokes. Spoon the mushrooms over the shrimp and artichokes.

6 Add the sherry and Worcestershire sauce to the cream sauce. Pour over the shrimp and artichokes. Sprinkle with the Parmesan cheese and dust with paprika.

7 Bake for 30 minutes, or until golden and bubbling. Serve hot.

▶ You can substitute canned artichoke hearts. Be sure to use those packed in water—not marinated artichoke hearts.

33

Hazelnut Cheesecake

SERVES 6
PREPARATION TIME: ABOUT 15 MINUTES
BAKING TIME: ABOUT 2 HOURS
COOLING TIME: 1 HOUR IN THE OVEN; 2 HOURS OUTSIDE THE OVEN

There is nothing as overwhelmingly wonderful as a cheesecake—smooth, rich, and oh-so-delicious. A real indulgence.

2 tablespoons unsalted butter, softened
Approximately 1/3 cup graham cracker crumbs
1 1/2 cups toasted, blanched hazelnuts or toasted, blanched almonds (see page 12)
2 pounds cream cheese, at room temperature
1/2 cup heavy cream
4 large eggs
1 3/4 cups granulated sugar
1 teaspoon pure vanilla extract

1 Preheat the oven to 300 degrees F. Assemble the *mise en place* trays for this recipe (see page 9). Generously grease a 9-by-3-inch-deep springform pan. Sprinkle the graham cracker crumbs over the pan, tilting it so that they cover the bottom and sides. Shake out the excess crumbs. Using 2 large sheets of aluminum foil, double-wrap the outside of the springform pan.

2 Place the nuts in a blender or food processor fitted with the metal blade. If you want the cheesecake to have a crunchy texture, process the nuts for about 20 seconds, until they are coarse-fine. If you want a smooth texture, process for about 1 minute, until they are almost paste-like.

3 Using an electric mixer set at low speed, beat the cream cheese, cream, eggs, sugar, and vanilla in a large bowl. As the ingredients blend, increase the speed to medium-high and continue beating until smooth. Add the nuts and beat until thoroughly incorporated.

4 Scrape the batter into the prepared pan and shake the pan gently to level the mixture. Set the pan inside a slightly wider pan and pour boiling water into the larger pan to a depth of about 1/2 inch, or until the water comes about halfway up the sides of the springform pan.

5 Bake for 2 hours. Turn off the oven and let the cake cool in the oven for 1 hour.

6 Remove the pans from the oven and lift the cake out of the water bath. Place on a wire rack and allow to sit for at least 2 hours.

7 Carefully remove the sides of the springform pan and set the cheesecake on a serving dish. Serve lukewarm or at room temperature, or refrigerate until about an hour before serving. Let the cake come to room temperature before serving.

▶ You can make this cheesecake in a 9-by-3-inch-deep cake pan. When the cheesecake is completely cool, invert it onto a serving plate by placing the plate over the top of the cake and turning both upside down.

▷ CRAIG CLAIBORNE: Hazelnut Cheesecake

A LATE-NIGHT SUPPER

Smoked Trout Mousse on Pumpernickel

Shrimp Ravioli with Tomatoes and Olives

*Chocolate Strudel and Poached Pears
with Cinnamon Sauce*

WINE SUGGESTIONS:

Cocktails or Champagne *(first course)*
Gavi or Frascati *(second course)*
Late Bottled Vintage Port *(dessert)*

Michael Lomonaco's menu is a perfect after-theater meal, as it can be prepared in advance. Since Chef Lomonaco's first passion was to be in the theater, after the theater is a particularly appropriate time to taste his food. He once thought he would have a career as an actor, but it is lucky for us that his equal fervor for fine food became the appetite that had to be fed.

Perhaps it is his love of traditional music that has allowed Michael to combine his taste for thoroughly modern cooking with the demands of convention at the world-famous '21' Club. I particularly like this menu because it allows you to offer hors d'oeuvres to your hungry guests as they arrive.

◁ MICHAEL LOMONACO: Smoked Trout Mousse on Pumpernickel
(recipe on page 38)

WHAT YOU CAN PREPARE AHEAD OF TIME

Up to 1 week ahead: Make the Shrimp Ravioli and freeze on a baking sheet until solid. Transfer to a rigid container, cover, and freeze. Just before serving, cook, without thawing, for 3 to 4 minutes.

Up to 3 days ahead: Poach the pears for the dessert. Cover and refrigerate in the poaching liquid. Bring to room temperature before serving.

The day before: Make the Smoked Trout Mousse. Cover and refrigerate. Let the mousse come to room temperature before piping. Make the Cinnamon Sauce. Cover and refrigerate.

Early in the day: Dice and drain the tomato garnish for the Smoked Trout Mousse. Make the sauce for the Shrimp Ravioli. Cover and refrigerate. Reheat before serving. Prepare the Shrimp Ravioli if not already made. Cover and refrigerate. Bake the Chocolate Strudel.

Smoked Trout Mousse on Pumpernickel

SERVES 6
PREPARATION TIME: ABOUT 20 MINUTES

You can use any fine smoked fish for this mousse. Since it multiplies easily, you could also serve it in an attractive bowl, with crackers, pita crisps, or toast points for an easy hors d'oeuvre for a large party.

1 tomato, cored, peeled, seeded, and diced
6 ounces boned, skinned, smoked trout fillets
3 tablespoons heavy cream
6 tablespoons unsalted butter, softened
6 slices pumpernickel bread
24 small, fresh dill sprigs

1 Assemble the *mise en place* trays for this recipe (see page 9).

2 Put the tomato in a strainer set over a plate to catch the juices. Set aside.

3 In a blender or a food processor fitted with the metal blade, combine the fish fillets and cream and process to a thick paste. Add the butter and pulse to combine. Scrape the mixture into a small bowl. Cover and refrigerate for 15 minutes.

4 Trim the crusts from the bread, and cut each slice into 4 triangles. Spoon the trout mousse into a pastry bag fitted with a star tip. Pipe an equal portion of mousse onto each bread triangle. Garnish each one with a sprig of dill and a few cubes of drained tomato.

Shrimp Ravioli with Tomatoes and Olives

SERVES 6
PREPARATION TIME: ABOUT 1 HOUR AND 15 MINUTES
COOKING TIME: ABOUT 25 MINUTES

This type of Italian tomato sauce is known as *puttanesca*, a word that, in polite company, translates to "streetwalker." It's a naughty name for a zesty and quite addictive sauce. Try it simply spooned over linguine or spaghetti.

SAUCE:

¼ cup plus 2 tablespoons olive oil
2 ounces canned anchovies, drained
½ to 1 teaspoon red pepper flakes, to taste
3 pounds very ripe plum tomatoes, cored, peeled, seeded, and chopped
2 tablespoons chopped shallots
2 tablespoons plus 1½ teaspoons chopped garlic
4 ounces Niçoise olives, pitted and chopped
¼ cup small capers, well drained
3 tablespoons chopped fresh flat-leaf parsley
1½ tablespoons chopped fresh basil
Freshly ground black pepper to taste

RAVIOLI:

1 pound large shrimp, peeled and deveined
1 tablespoon plus 1½ teaspoons olive oil
3 tablespoons chopped shallots
1½ teaspoons chopped garlic
3 tablespoons chopped fresh flat-leaf parsley
3 tablespoons chopped fresh cilantro
1½ tablespoons chopped fresh thyme
Salt and freshly ground black pepper to taste
1 egg white, lightly beaten
1 package wonton wrappers (about 50 wrappers)

1 Assemble the *mise en place* trays for this recipe (see page 9).

2 To make the sauce, heat the oil in a large sauté pan over medium heat. Add the anchovies and red pepper flakes and cook for about 4 minutes or until the anchovies "melt."

3 Add the tomatoes and cook, stirring occasionally, for 5 to 10 minutes, until very soft. Stir in the shallots, garlic,

▷ MICHAEL LOMONACO: Shrimp Ravioli with Tomatoes and Olives

olives, capers, parsley, and basil. Season to taste with pepper. Remove the pan from the heat and set aside.

4 To make the ravioli filling, use a sharp knife to cut the shrimp into nuggets the size of peas.

5 In a medium-sized sauté pan, heat the oil over medium heat. Add the shrimp and sauté for 2 minutes, or until just cooked. Stir in the shallots, garlic, parsley, cilantro, and thyme. Season to taste with salt and pepper. Remove from the heat and allow to cool (about 20 minutes).

6 When the shrimp mixture is cool, stir in the egg white.

7 Separate the wonton wrappers. Using a small pastry brush dipped in cold water, moisten the edges of 1 wonton wrapper. Place 1 teaspoon of the cooled shrimp mixture in the center. Fold over diagonally into a triangle and pinch the edges together to seal. Put the ravioli on a parchment-lined baking sheet and continue making ravioli until all the wrappers are used.

8 Meanwhile, in a large pot, bring 2 quarts of water to a boil over high heat. When boiling, lightly salt the water.

9 Drop the ravioli into the boiling water one by one. Stir gently to prevent sticking and return the water to a slow boil. Cook for 1 to 2 minutes, until the ravioli bob to the surface of the pot. Lift the ravioli out of the water with a slotted spoon and carefully put into a colander to drain.

10 While the ravioli are cooking, warm the sauce over low heat.

11 Place the ravioli on a warm serving platter, and spoon the warm sauce over the top. Serve immediately.

▶ **The ravioli could also be made with traditional pasta dough, but the wonton wrappers make an especially easy preparation.**

Chocolate Strudel and Poached Pears with Cinnamon Sauce

SERVES 6
PREPARATION TIME: ABOUT 45 MINUTES
COOKING AND BAKING TIME: ABOUT 50 MINUTES

Each component of this dessert can be prepared in advance. The pears can be poached and the strudel rolled so that the dessert can be assembled just before serving.

3 ripe Bosc pears, peeled, cored, and halved lengthwise
1½ cups water
¾ cup semisweet white wine, such as Muscat de Beaumes-de-Venise or Muscat from Northern Italy
3 tablespoons granulated sugar
1 teaspoon ground cinnamon
6 sheets frozen filo pastry, thawed according to package directions
½ cup unsalted butter, melted
¼ cup chopped walnuts
6 ounces bittersweet chocolate, finely chopped
1 tablespoon unsweetened cocoa powder
Cinnamon Sauce (recipe follows)
6 fresh mint sprigs

1 Assemble the *mise en place* trays for this recipe (see page 9).

2 In a medium-sized, nonreactive saucepan, combine the pears, water, wine, sugar, and cinnamon, and bring to a boil over high heat. Reduce the heat to low and simmer for 10 to 12 minutes, or until the pears are tender but not soft. Remove from heat and let the pears cool in the liquid.

3 Preheat the oven to 375 degrees F.

4 Lay 1 filo sheet on a work surface. Lightly brush it with melted butter, and sprinkle with 1 tablespoon of the walnuts. Lay another filo sheet on top, brush with butter and sprinkle with walnuts. Repeat the layering process with the remaining sheets, leaving the top sheet plain.

5 Sprinkle the chopped chocolate evenly over the top sheet of filo and then sprinkle with the cocoa powder. Starting from a long side, roll up jelly-roll fashion into a log. Brush with the remaining melted butter.

6 Transfer the strudel to a baking sheet. Bake for about 20 minutes, or until golden. Cool on the baking sheet for about 10 minutes.

7 Using a serrated knife, cut the strudel into slices no more than 1/2 inch thick.

8 Drain the pears well. Cut each half lengthwise from the stem end into thin slices, keeping it intact at the stem end.

9 Spoon the Cinnamon Sauce onto 6 dessert plates. Fan a pear half out on each plate. Place a strudel slice beside each pear. Garnish each plate with a mint sprig and serve.

▶ **When working with filo pastry, it is important to keep the sheets you are not using covered with a damp dish towel or cloth. Wrap unused filo well in plastic and foil and freeze.**

CINNAMON SAUCE
MAKES ABOUT 3/4 CUP

1 large egg yolk, at room temperature
2 tablespoons granulated sugar
1/2 cup milk
1/4 teaspoon ground cinnamon

1 In a medium-sized bowl, whisk together the egg yolk, sugar, and cinnamon until smooth.

2 Heat the milk in the top half of a double boiler until scalded (just below a boil). Gradually add the milk to the egg mixture, whisking constantly. Return the mixture to the double boiler and cook over hot water, whisking constantly, for 2 to 3 minutes until thick enough to coat the back of a spoon. Remove the pan from the heat and allow to cool. Use as soon as it's cool, or cover and refrigerate until ready to serve.

MICHAEL LOMONACO: **Chocolate Strudel and Poached Pears with Cinnamon Sauce**

A Dinner Filled with Remembrances of The Flavors of the South of France

Provençal Vegetable Tart with Seared Tuna

Striped Bass with Artichokes and Aïoli

Vanilla Custard with Maple-Roasted Peanuts

Wine Suggestions:

White Côtes du Rhône or Rosé *(first course)*

Sauvignon Blanc *(second course)*

Tawny Port *(dessert)*

What You Can Prepare Ahead of Time

Up to 2 days ahead: Make the Aïoli for the Striped Bass with Artichokes and Aïoli. Cover and refrigerate.

Early in the day: Cook the artichokes for both the Provençal Vegetable Tart and the Striped Bass. Cover and store at cool room temperature. Prepare the remaining components for the Provençal Vegetable Tart, except the tuna. Cover the vegetables and refrigerate. Wrap the salad and herbs in damp paper towels and refrigerate. Wrap the pastry in wax paper and refrigerate. Bake the Vanilla Custards. Cover and refrigerate. Chop the peanuts.

Up to 1 hour before the party: Cook the tuna for the Provençal Vegetable Tart.

Wayne Nish prepared this menu some years ago, when he was the executive chef at La Colombe d'Or Restaurant in New York City. After the wonderful class, we all went home inspired to recapture his wonderful flavors and to bring a taste of France into our American kitchens.

Chef Nish subsequently went on to become chef and co-owner of the critically acclaimed March Restaurant, where he added other more exotic flavors to his menu. Recently he returned to the flavors of France when he became co-owner of La Colombe d'Or, while retaining his interest at March. This early menu reflects some of Wayne's long-held food enthusiasms. I think that you will find that the flavors and colors—which echo each other from appetizer to entrée—make this challenging meal a memorable one.

◁ **WAYNE NISH: Provençal Vegetable Tart with Seared Tuna** (recipe on page 44)

Provençal Vegetable Tart with Seared Tuna

SERVES 6
PREPARATION TIME: ABOUT 1 HOUR AND 30 MINUTES
COOKING TIME: ABOUT 30 MINUTES
CHILLING TIME (PASTRY ONLY): 1 HOUR AND 30 MINUTES

The simple tastes of Provence combine in an unusual fashion to make this a very contemporary dish. Since all of the components can be prepared in advance, it is an especially appealing appetizer for the busy cook.

TART PASTRY:

¾ cup unsalted butter
½ cup solid vegetable shortening
1½ cups sifted all-purpose flour
½ teaspoon kosher salt
½ cup ice water

TOPPING:

3 baby artichokes, trimmed, or artichoke hearts (not marinated)
1 large ripe tomato, cored, peeled, seeded, and cut into strips 1 to 1½ inches long
2 teaspoons chopped fresh thyme
Salt and freshly ground black pepper to taste
1 clove garlic, sliced
½ lemon, quartered
1 cup plus 3 tablespoons extra-virgin olive oil
1 large zucchini, trimmed, cored, and cut into 2-inch long *bâtonnets*
½ cup fresh peas or fava beans
½ cup tomato juice
12 ounces sashimi-quality tuna, about 1 inch thick, cut into slices, 2-inches by 2-inches

SALAD:

2 cups mesclun or other baby salad greens, rinsed and dried
1 tablespoon chopped fresh basil leaves
1 tablespoon chopped fresh tarragon leaves
1 tablespoon chopped fresh parsley leaves
1 tablespoon chopped fresh chives
1 tablespoon chopped fresh chervil sprigs

■ Special Equipment: 3-inch round cookie cutter

1 Assemble the *mise en place* trays for this recipe (see page 9).

2 To make the tart pastry, cut the butter and shortening into tablespoon-sized pieces. Wrap the butter and shortening separately in plastic wrap and freeze for 30 minutes.

3 Combine the flour and salt in the bowl of a food processor fitted with the metal blade. Add the chilled butter and pulse until the mixture is the consistency of coarse meal. Add the shortening and pulse for 3 to 4 seconds longer.

4 With the motor running, slowly add the ice water and process until the dough comes together in a smooth, sticky ball. Wrap in plastic wrap and refrigerate for 1 hour.

5 Roll out the dough between 2 sheets of plastic wrap to a rectangle about ¼ inch thick. Place on a baking sheet and freeze for about 30 minutes.

6 Preheat the oven to 350 degrees F.

7 Using a 3-inch round cookie cutter, cut the dough into 6 circles. Place on an ungreased baking sheet. Cover the circles with parchment paper, waxed paper, or foil, and set another baking sheet on top of pastry circles. Bake for 7 minutes. Remove the top baking sheet and the paper and bake for 3 or 4 minutes longer. Turn the pastries over and bake for another 3 to 4 minutes or until the pastry is golden. Remove to a wire rack to cool. Reduce the oven temperature to 300 degrees F.

8 To prepare the topping, cook the artichokes in boiling salted water for 10 minutes, or until tender. Drain well and let cool.

9 In a small bowl, combine the tomato strips, 1 teaspoon of the thyme, and salt and pepper to taste. Set aside.

10 Cut the artichokes in half lengthwise. Place in a small, ovenproof dish and add the garlic, the remaining 1 teaspoon thyme, the lemon quarters, and salt and pepper to taste. Cover tightly with aluminum foil and bake for 10 minutes. Uncover and let cool.

11 Meanwhile, in small sauté pan, heat 1 teaspoon of the olive oil over medium heat. Add the zucchini, season to taste with salt and pepper, and sauté for 2 minutes, or until just beginning to color. Remove from the heat and set aside.

▷ WAYNE NISH: Provençal Vegetable Tart with Seared Tuna

12 Blanch the peas or fava beans in boiling salted water for 30 seconds. Drain and refresh under cold running water. Set aside. (If using fava beans, peel them after blanching.)

13 Place the tomato juice in a blender with the motor running, and add 1 cup of olive oil in a slow, steady stream until fully emulsified. Season to taste with salt and pepper. Set aside.

14 In a large, heavy sauté pan, heat 1 tablespoon of the oil over medium heat. Sear the tuna for 15 to 20 seconds on all sides; it should be rare in the middle. Transfer to a cutting board and allow to cool.

15 Cut the tuna into long, thin slices about ¼ to ⅛ inch thick. Season the slices lightly with the remaining 1 tablespoon plus 2 teaspoons olive oil and salt.

16 To make the salad, toss the salad greens with the fresh herbs.

17 Place a pastry disk in the center of each appetizer plate. Arrange the tomato, artichokes, peas or beans, and zucchini on the disks and top each one with a small mound of the herb salad. Drape the sliced tuna over the salad, and drizzle with the tomato and oil dressing. Serve at once.

▶ **Freshness is always important when purchasing fish. Sashimi-quality tuna refers to the freshest, highest-quality tuna available, because it is the tuna used for Japanese sashimi, fish served raw. For this recipe, buy the very best tuna you can find.**

Striped Bass with Artichokes and Aïoli

SERVES 6
PREPARATION TIME: ABOUT 45 MINUTES
COOKING TIME: ABOUT 55 MINUTES
RESTING TIME (AIOLI ONLY): 8 HOURS

Aïoli is the richly flavored garlic mayonnaise favored throughout Provence as an accompaniment to lightly steamed or grilled poultry, fish, or fresh vegetables. Here, it highlights a simply cooked bass.

6 small artichokes, trimmed, or large artichoke hearts (not marinated)
1 whole head garlic, halved crosswise
1 lemon, quartered
1 tablespoon chopped fresh thyme
Salt and freshly ground black pepper to taste
6 six-ounce striped bass fillets with skin
Kosher salt to taste
¼ cup extra-virgin olive oil
Aïoli (recipe follows)

1 Preheat the oven to 300 degrees F. Assemble the *mise en place* trays for this recipe (see page 9).

2 Cook the artichokes in boiling, salted water for 12 to 15 minutes, or until tender. Drain and let cool slightly.

3 Cut the artichokes in half lengthwise. Place the artichokes, garlic, lemon, thyme, and salt and pepper to taste in a small ovenproof dish. Cover tightly with aluminum foil and bake for 20 minutes. Uncover and set aside to cool.

4 Heat 2 ten-inch, medium-weight skillets over medium-high heat for 4 to 5 minutes.

5 Lightly season both sides of the fish with kosher salt.

6 Pour half the olive oil into each pan. Place 3 of the fish fillets in each pan, skin-side down. Cover the pan with a lid or another skillet laid upside down so that it resembles a dome. Cook the fish for 6 minutes, without turning. Transfer to paper towels to drain.

7 Place a fish fillet in the center of each warm dinner plate. Lay 2 artichoke halves next to each one. Spoon Aïoli over all, or place on one side of the plate, and pass the remaining Aïoli on the side.

▶ **The striped bass can be replaced with red snapper or another firm-fleshed saltwater fish.**

▷ WAYNE NISH: Striped Bass with Artichokes and Aïoli

AÏOLI

MAKES ABOUT 2⅔ CUPS

18 cloves garlic, 6 cloves minced and 12 left whole
¾ cup extra-virgin olive oil
1½ cups peanut oil
6 large egg yolks
¼ cup heavy cream
3 tablespoons fresh lemon juice
2 teaspoons kosher salt

1 In a small sauté pan, combine the whole garlic cloves and 2 tablespoons olive oil. Cover and cook over very low heat, stirring occasionally, for about 15 minutes, or until the garlic is very soft.

2 In a blender, combine the softened garlic and minced fresh garlic with 4 tablespoons peanut oil and blend until smooth. Set aside.

3 In a medium-sized glass or ceramic bowl, beat the egg yolks with a hand-held electric mixer set at high speed until well blended. While continuing to beat, gradually add ½ cup of the remaining peanut oil in a slow, steady stream until completely emulsified. Stir in the cream and lemon juice and transfer the mixture to a heavy saucepan. Cook over low heat just until bubbles form around the edges. Remove from heat and let the mixture stand for 2 to 3 minutes (this will kill any bacteria in the raw eggs). Return the mixture to the bowl and gradually whisk in the remaining ¾ cup peanut oil until incorportaed.

4 Whisk in the garlic puree and salt. Using the mixer set at medium speed, beat in the remaining 10 tablespoons olive oil a little at a time until incorporated.

5 Cover and refrigerate for at least 8 hours before using. Whisk well before serving.

Vanilla Custard with Maple-Roasted Peanuts

SERVES 6
PREPARATION TIME: ABOUT 20 MINUTES
COOKING AND BAKING TIME: 35 TO 40 MINUTES

These simple baked custards, with their pure, uncomplicated flavors, are the perfect ending to an elaborate meal.

4 cups milk
¾ cup granulated sugar
8 large egg yolks
2 tablespoons pure vanilla extract
⅛ teaspoon salt
1 cup high-quality pure maple syrup
4 ounces maple-roasted peanuts, coarsely chopped

■ Special Equipment: 6 six-ounce ramekins or custard cups

1 Assemble the *mise en place* trays for this recipe (see page 9).

2 In a medium-sized, heavy saucepan, combine the milk and sugar. Cook over low heat, stirring for 5 minutes, or until the sugar is dissolved. Do not allow to boil. Transfer to a large bowl and let cool to room temperature.

3 Whisk the egg yolks, vanilla extract, and salt into the milk mixture. Strain through a fine strainer. Pour the custard into 6 six-ounce shallow ramekins or custard cups.

4 Place the cups in a large, flat roasting pan. Add enough hot water to come about ½ inch up the sides of the cups. Bake for 35 to 40 minutes, or until the custard is barely set. Remove from the oven and allow to cool in the water bath for about 5 minutes before lifting from the roasting pan and cooling completely on the counter.

5 To serve, drizzle about 2½ tablespoons of the maple syrup over each custard and sprinkle each with about 2 tablespoons of the peanuts.

▶ **The peanuts can be replaced with any glazed, roasted nuts.**

▶ **Place a tea towel or dish towel on the bottom of a roasting pan, under the custard cups, to prevent them from moving around while cooking.**

◁ WAYNE NISH: Vanilla Custard with Maple-Roasted Peanuts

A Leisurely Sunday Lunch

Spring Vegetable Stew with Pesto

*Creamy Polenta with Roasted Wild Mushrooms
and Fried Sage Leaves*

Apricot and Ginger Crisp

Wine Suggestions:

Sauvignon Blanc *(first course)*

Reserve Chardonnay *(second course)*

Vin Santo or Calvados *(dessert)*

What You Can Prepare Ahead of Time

Up to 1 week ahead: Prepare the Vegetable Stock for the Spring Vegetable Stew (if making your own). Prepare the Chicken Stock for the Creamy Polenta (if making your own).

Up to 2 days ahead: Make the Pesto for the Spring Vegetable Stew. Cover and refrigerate.

Early in the day: Prepare all the components for the Spring Vegetable Stew (including the Pesto, if not already made). Cover and refrigerate. Bake the Apricot and Ginger Crisp. Reheat in a 300-degree F. oven for 10 minutes before serving.

Up to 1 hour before the party: Fry the Sage Leaves for the Creamy Polenta. Store, uncovered, at room temperature. Combine the mushrooms with the flavorings for the Creamy Polenta.

Bradley Ogden gives us a menu filled with a bounty of beautifully flavored vegetables. You will feel as though you have visited a deluxe farmer's market, as Chef Ogden has captured the down-home feeling as well as the lushness of freshly picked produce that such markets offer the city-dweller. Each course can stand on its own, but, in combination, the menu offers a wonderful contrast of flavors and textures.

Bradley Ogden first visited De Gustibus when he was executive chef at Campton Place in San Francisco, and he was quite the rising star of the contemporary American kitchen. He subsequently opened his own Lark Creek Inn in Larkspur, California, where he is able to showcase his ability to combine home-style food with contemporary taste.

◁ Bradley Ogden: Creamy Polenta with Roasted Wild Mushrooms and Fried Sage Leaves (recipe on page 54)

Spring Vegetable Stew with Pesto

You would have to be Peter Rabbit to make a fresher tasting stew. It's light enough to make a delightful first course, but served with homemade bread, it makes a lovely spring lunch.

1 cup fresh fava beans (1 pound unshelled)
1/2 cup fresh peas (8 ounces unshelled)
1 small head broccoli, divided into small florets (about 2 cups)
5 cups Vegetable Stock (see page 14)
1 pound thick asparagus spears, peeled and cut into 2-inch pieces (about 2 cups)
1 medium fennel bulb, trimmed, cored, and cut into 1-inch dice (about 1 1/2 cups)
2 tomatoes, cored, peeled, seeded, and diced
1 yellow squash, trimmed, peeled, and cut into 1/4-inch-thick slices (about 2 cups)
3/4 pound small curly spinach leaves, trimmed, rinsed, and dried
Kosher salt and freshly ground black pepper to taste
1/3 cup fresh chervil leaves
2 tablespoons fresh tarragon leaves
Pesto (recipe follows)

1 Assemble the *mise en place* trays for this recipe (see page 9).

2 In a large saucepan of lightly salted, boiling water, cook the fava beans for 2 minutes, or until just tender. Using a strainer or slotted spoon, remove the beans from the boiling water. Refresh under cold running water and drain well. Remove the skins from the beans and discard. Set the beans aside.

3 Add the peas and broccoli florets to the boiling water and cook for 30 seconds. Drain, rinse under cold running water, and drain well. Set aside.

4 In a large pot, bring the stock to a boil over high heat. Add the asparagus and fennel and cook for 30 seconds.

5 Add the fava beans, peas, broccoli, and the remaining vegetables and cook for 3 minutes, or until the spinach has wilted; do not overcook. Season to taste with salt and pepper. Stir in the chervil and tarragon.

6 Ladle the stew into 6 warm, shallow soup bowls. Generously spoon the Pesto over the top, and serve immediately.

▶ Use any fresh spring vegetables in this stew—for example, black-eyed peas could replace the peas. Young bitter greens, such as mustard and kale, could be added or could replace the spinach. Fresh corn kernels could also be used later in the season, when corn is at its most succulent.

PESTO
MAKES ABOUT 1 CUP

2 tablespoons ground almonds
1/2 cup loosely packed fresh basil leaves
2 tablespoons chopped fresh flat-leaf parsley
1/2 teaspoon minced garlic
1/4 cup olive oil
2 teaspoons balsamic vinegar
1 teaspoon fresh lemon juice
2 tablespoons freshly grated Parmesan cheese
Kosher salt and freshly cracked black pepper to taste

1 Combine the almonds, basil, parsley, garlic, and olive oil in a blender or food processor fitted with the metal blade and process until smooth.

2 Transfer the puree to a glass or ceramic bowl. Stir in the vinegar, lemon juice, Parmesan cheese, and salt and pepper to taste. Cover and let rest at room temperature for several hours until ready to serve.

▶ **An easy way to peel fresh fava beans is, working down the pod, snap to release each fava bean and push it out with thumb and forefinger.**

▷ BRADLEY OGDEN: *Spring Vegetable Stew with Pesto*

Creamy Polenta with Roasted Wild Mushrooms and Fried Sage Leaves

The earthy mushrooms add extra body and fullness to the polenta. Without the mushrooms, the rich polenta is a terrific side dish, excellent served with a plate of grilled vegetables.

1½ cups water
1½ cups Chicken Stock (see page 13)
9 cloves garlic, 8 cloves sliced, 1 clove minced
¾ cup polenta
6 cups any combination of flavorful mushrooms, such as shiitakes, morels, chanterelles, Italian browns, or cèpes, trimmed
4½ tablespoons olive oil
4½ tablespoons balsamic vinegar
3 sprigs fresh thyme
3 sprigs fresh rosemary
Kosher salt and freshly cracked black pepper to taste
3 tablespoons unsalted butter
⅔ cup crème fraîche, at room temperature
¼ cup freshly grated, aged Monterey Jack cheese
¼ cup freshly grated Parmesan cheese
Fried Sage Leaves (recipe follows)

1 Preheat the oven to 350 degrees F. Assemble the *mise en place* trays for this recipe (see page 9).

2 In a medium-sized, heavy-bottomed, ovenproof saucepan, bring the water, stock, and minced garlic to a full boil over high heat. Slowly whisk in the polenta. Reduce the heat and cook for 5 minutes, stirring constantly with a wooden spoon. Cover, transfer to the oven, and bake for 45 minutes, stirring 2 or 3 times to prevent sticking.

3 Meanwhile, combine the mushrooms, sliced garlic, olive oil, vinegar, thyme, rosemary, and salt and pepper to taste in a shallow roasting pan. About 20 minutes before the polenta is ready, place the pan on a rack in the lower half of the oven and roast for 20 minutes, or until lightly browned and tender.

4 Remove the polenta and mushrooms from the oven. Beat the butter, crème fraîche, and cheeses into the polenta. Taste and adjust the seasoning with salt and pepper.

5 Spoon the polenta onto 6 warm plates. Spoon the mushrooms over the polenta. Garnish with the Fried Sage Leaves and serve immediately.

▶ Crème fraîche is available in the refrigerated foods section of specialty stores and some supermarkets.

▶ Polenta is both Italian cornmeal and the dish made from it. It is served as a main course or side dish, depending on the ingredients added to it and the rest of the menu. In the first stages of cooking, it is important to stir polenta continuously. In Italy, many cooks use a stick to stir polenta, but a long-handled wooden spoon works fine.

FRIED SAGE LEAVES
MAKES ABOUT ⅔ CUP

1 cup peanut oil
⅔ cup fresh sage leaves
Salt to taste

1 In a small sauté pan, heat the oil over high heat until very hot. Add a few sage leaves and fry for about 45 seconds, until the leaves are crisp and the edges begin to curl. Using a slotted spoon or long-handled strainer, remove the crisp leaves and drain on paper towels. Continue frying until all leaves are cooked.

2 Lightly sprinkle each batch of leaves with salt as they are fried. Store at room temperature until ready to use.

▶ Wipe the sage leaves clean with a paper towel. If you must wash them, be sure they are completely dry before frying.

Apricot and Ginger Crisp

This is a real home-style dessert that is always a hit. You can replace the apricots with ripe peaches or nectarines, depending on what is best in the market.

1/3 cup packed light brown sugar
3/4 cup plus 3 tablespoons all-purpose flour
1/4 cup grated fresh ginger
1 1/4 teaspoons ground cinnamon
Grated zest of 1 lemon
5 cups fresh apricot halves (about 2 pounds)
2/3 cup packed dark brown sugar
1/4 teaspoon salt
1/8 teaspoon ground ginger
6 tablespoons unsalted butter, cut into 1-inch pieces and chilled
Vanilla ice cream, for serving (optional)

1 Preheat oven to 375 degrees F. Assemble the *mise en place* trays for this recipe (see page 9).

2 In a large bowl, combine the light brown sugar, 3 tablespoons of the flour, the grated ginger, 1 teaspoon of the cinnamon, and the lemon zest. Add the apricots and toss gently until lightly coated. Set aside.

3 In another bowl, combine the remaining 3/4 cup flour and 1/4 teaspoon cinnamon with the dark brown sugar, salt, and ground ginger. Cut in the butter until the mixture resembles coarse meal.

4 Arrange the apricots, cut side down, in a single layer in the bottom of a 9- by 13-inch glass or ceramic baking dish. Sprinkle the topping evenly over the fruit. Bake for 20 to 30 minutes, or until the fruit is soft and the topping is crisp.

5 Serve warm, with ice cream if desired.

BRADLEY OGDEN: **Apricot and Ginger Crisp**

A PERFECT DINNER PARTY

Open Ravioli of Wild Mushrooms and
Caramelized Onion

Seared "Steak-Cut" Haddock with
Lentil Ragout and Citrus Shallot Sauce

Banana-Pecan Strudel with
Raisin Brandy Cream

WINE SUGGESTIONS:

White Burgundy *(first and second course)*
Tawny Port *(dessert)*

WHAT YOU CAN PREPARE AHEAD OF TIME

Up to 1 week ahead: Prepare the Chicken Stock for the Open Ravioli and "Steak-Cut" Haddock (if making your own). Make the Chive Oil. Store in a tightly covered, glass container in a cool, dark place.

Up to 3 days before: Prepare the Tomato Compote through Step 1. Cover and refrigerate. Add the herbs and reheat just before serving.

Early in the day: Make the pasta squares for the Open Ravioli. Wrap tightly and store at room temperature. Prepare the caramelized onions and mushroom mixture for the Open Ravioli. Cover and store at room temperature. Reheat just before serving. Prepare the Lentil Ragout for the "Steak-Cut" Haddock. Cover and store at cool room temperature. Reheat just before serving. Soak the raisins for the Banana-Pecan Strudel. Assemble the strudels. Cover and refrigerate. Bake just before serving.

Charlie Palmer represents the ideal of a truly great New American chef. He combines his classical training and refined taste with impeccably chosen ingredients and a genuine love of food.

De Gustibus students first met Chef Palmer when he was executive chef at the River Cafe in Brooklyn, New York. We have watched him soar at his own acclaimed restaurant, Aureole, in Manhattan. He has taught many classes and never fails to thrill his adoring fans.

This menu presents a perfect balance of flavor, color, and texture. It is extravagant in feeling but easy to execute in the home kitchen, allowing the home cook to receive the raves usually reserved for Charlie.

◁ CHARLES PALMER: Banana-Pecan Strudel with Raisin Brandy Cream
(recipe on page 61)

Open Ravioli of Wild Mushrooms and Caramelized Onion

SERVES 6
PREPARATION TIME: ABOUT 2 HOURS
COOKING TIME: ABOUT 1 HOUR

This beautiful first course is not as difficult as first glance might indicate. Much can be done in advance to rate those "oohs" and "ahs" at the table.

PASTA:

1 cup semolina flour
1 cup bread flour
2 large eggs
3 tablespoons olive oil
1 teaspoon salt, or more to taste
2 tablespoons chopped fresh parsley
Approximately 3 tablespoons ice water

FILLING:

1 tablespoon olive oil
1 large Spanish onion, halved and thinly sliced
1 cup sliced chanterelle mushrooms
1 cup coarsely chopped oyster mushrooms
Salt to taste
¾ cup Chicken Stock (see page 13)
1 tablespoon unsalted butter
1 tablespoon plus 1 teaspoon chopped fresh parsley
2 teaspoons chopped fresh chives
Freshly ground black pepper to taste
Tomato Compote (recipe follows)
Chive Oil (recipe follows)
12 small chive stalks

■ Special Equipment: pasta machine (optional)

1 Assemble the *mise en place* trays for this recipe (see page 9).

2 To make the pasta, in the bowl of a heavy-duty mixer, combine the flours, eggs, olive oil, and 1 teaspoon salt. Beat at low speed until mixed. Add the parsley, increase the speed to medium, and continue to beat until the dough forms a smooth ball. If the dough seems dry, add cold water, 1 teaspoon at a time.

3 Using a pasta machine, roll the dough into thin sheets with the machine on the next-to-last setting. Alternately, roll out into a thin sheet on a lightly floured surface.

CHARLES PALMER: **Open Ravioli of Wild Mushrooms and Caramelized Onion**

4 Cut the pasta dough into twelve 4-by-4-inch squares. Stack the squares, placing a sheet of plastic wrap or parchment paper between each square, and wrap the stack in parchment or waxed paper. Set aside. Reserve the remaining dough for another use.

5 To make the filling, in a large non-stick sauté pan, heat the olive oil over medium heat. Add the onions, reduce the heat to low and cook, covered, for 10 minutes. Raise the heat to medium-low and cook, uncovered, for 10 to 15 minutes longer, or until the onions are well caramelized.

Using a slotted spoon, remove the onions from the pan and set aside.

6 Add the mushrooms to the pan and sprinkle lightly with salt. Raise the heat to medium and cook for 1 minute, or until well coated with the pan juices. Stir in the Chicken Stock and butter. Cook, stirring occasionally, for about 8 minutes, or until the mushrooms are tender and the liquid has reduced to a rich sauce.

7 Stir in the reserved caramelized onions, 1 teaspoon parsley, and the chopped chives. Season to taste with salt and pepper. Remove from the heat and cover to keep warm.

8 Meanwhile, in a large saucepan, bring 2 quarts of water to a boil over high heat. Salt lightly.

9 Add the pasta squares to the boiling water and cook for 1 minute, or until *al dente*. Drain well.

10 Spoon the mushroom mixture into the bottom of each of 6 shallow soup bowls. Place one pasta square in each bowl over the mushroom mixture. Spoon the Tomato Compote on top of the ravioli and drizzle the Chive Oil on top. Garnish with chive stalks and the remaining 1 tablespoon parsley, and serve immediately.

▶ **If not using pasta dough immediately, wrap it tightly in plastic and let it rest at room temperature. Do not refrigerate, and do not allow it to sit for more than three hours or dough will toughen and be unusable. You may, however, cut the pasta in squares, wrap them as instructed in the recipe, and let them sit at room temperature for up to 8 hours.**

▶ **To save time, purchase commercially prepared pasta sheets and cut into desired size. If these are not available, you could use dried lasagna noodles. Cook as directed on the package and cut into four-inch squares.**

TOMATO COMPOTE
MAKES ABOUT 1 CUP

1 1/2 cups cored, peeled, seeded, and chopped ripe tomatoes
1 tablespoon chopped sun-dried tomatoes packed in oil, drained
1 tablespoon olive oil
1/4 teaspoon red pepper flakes, or to taste
Salt and freshly ground black pepper to taste
2 tablespoons chopped fresh basil
2 tablespoons chopped fresh chives

1 In a small saucepan, combine the fresh and sun-dried tomatoes. Stir in the olive oil, red pepper flakes, and salt and pepper to taste, and bring to a simmer over medium heat. Reduce the heat and cook gently for 15 to 20 minutes, until thickened.

2 Remove from the heat and stir in the basil and chives. Serve warm.

CHIVE OIL
MAKES ABOUT 1/2 CUP

2 ounces fresh chives
1 1/2 teaspoons cold water
1/2 cup grapeseed oil
Kosher salt and freshly ground black pepper to taste

1 Blanch the chives in a small pan of boiling water for 30 seconds. Drain immediately and refresh under cold running water. Pat dry and roughly chop.

2 Place the chives in a blender, add the cold water and blend until just pureed. Do not overprocess or the bright green color will fade. Scrape the puree into a small glass or ceramic bowl. Whisk in the oil and season to taste with salt and pepper. Use right away or cover tightly and store in a cool, dark place.

Seared "Steak-Cut" Haddock with Lentil Ragout and Citrus Shallot Sauce

In this recipe, Charlie treats the fish as though it were a piece of steak. The interesting combination of textures and flavors creates a contemporary taste for this mild, low-fat fish.

RAGOUT:

6 sprigs fresh parsley
4 sprigs fresh thyme
1 clove garlic
6 black peppercorns
2 tablespoons olive oil
3/4 cup diced onions
1/2 cup diced carrots
1 cup green French lentils (Le Puy lentils), picked through, rinsed, and drained
2 cups Chicken Stock (see page 13)
1/2 cup peeled, sliced, cooked, small new potatoes
Salt and freshly ground black pepper to taste

HADDOCK:

2 tablespoons grapeseed oil
Salt and freshly ground black pepper to taste
6 six-ounce, thick-cut, fresh haddock steaks (1 1/4 to 1 1/2 inches thick)
3 tablespoons minced shallots
3 tablespoons unsalted butter
1 tablespoon olive oil
1 1/4 cups Chicken Stock (see page 13)
Zest and juice of 2 lemons
1 tablespoon minced fresh parsley
1 teaspoon minced fresh thyme

1 Assemble the *mise en place* trays for this recipe (see page 9).

2 To make the ragout, wrap the parsley and thyme sprigs, garlic, and peppercorns in a cheesecloth bag and tie securely to make an herb sachet.

3 In a medium-sized saucepan, heat the olive oil over medium-high heat. Add the onions and carrots and cook for 2 minutes. Add the lentils and cook for 2 minutes. Add the stock and herb sachet and bring to a simmer. Simmer

for 20 to 30 minutes, until all the liquid has been absorbed and the lentils are tender. Remove from the heat and discard the sachet. Stir in the potatoes, season to taste with salt and pepper, and cover to keep warm.

4 To prepare the haddock, heat the grapeseed oil in a large, nonstick skillet over medium-high heat. Season the haddock steaks with salt and pepper to taste and place in the hot pan. Cook for 5 to 7 minutes, or until golden brown and lightly crusted on the bottom. Turn the fish and sear the other side. Transfer to a plate and cover with aluminum foil to keep warm.

CHARLES PALMER: Seared "Steak-Cut" Haddock with Lentil Ragout and Citrus Shallot Sauce

5 Reduce the heat to medium and add the shallots and butter to the pan. Cook for 2 minutes, or until the butter starts to brown and foam. Add the olive oil and stock and cook, stirring occasionally, for 10 minutes, or until the liquid is reduced by half. Whisk in the lemon juice and zest and minced herbs. Adjust the seasoning with salt and pepper.

6 Spoon equal portions of Lentil Ragout onto 6 warm dinner plates. Place the haddock steaks on the plates and spoon the pan sauce over and around the fish.

Banana-Pecan Strudel with Raisin Brandy Cream

SERVES 6 (12 STRUDELS)
PREPARATION TIME: ABOUT 20 MINUTES
COOKING AND BAKING TIME: 20 TO 25 MINUTES
SOAKING TIME (RAISINS ONLY): 1 HOUR

An old-fashioned dessert idea is made modern here with an unusual filling.

1/4 cup raisins
1/2 cup brandy
6 ripe bananas
3/4 cup plus 2 tablespoons granulated sugar
1 1/2 cups chopped, toasted pecans (see page 12)
1/2 cup packed dark brown sugar
18 sheets frozen filo pastry, thawed
3/4 cup clarified butter (see page 12)
1 1/2 cups heavy cream
Confectioners' sugar, for dusting

1 Preheat the broiler. Assemble the *mise en place* trays for this recipe (see page 9). Line 2 baking sheets with parchment.

2 Combine the raisins and brandy in a small glass or ceramic bowl and let soak for 1 hour.

3 Meanwhile, peel the bananas and cut in half lengthwise. Cut crosswise into 1-inch pieces. Place the bananas on one of the prepared baking sheets and sprinkle with 1/2 cup of the granulated sugar. Place under the broiler for about 5 minutes, until the sugar caramelizes, watching carefully to insure that it does not burn. Cool to room temperature. When cool, gently lift the bananas from the baking sheet.

4 Preheat the oven to 350 degrees F.

5 In a bowl, combine the bananas, pecans, 1/4 cup of the granulated sugar and the brown sugar. Stir well.

6 Lay 6 sheets of the filo pastry on a work surface. Lightly brush with clarified butter. Lay another filo sheet on top of each and brush with butter. Lay the remaining filo sheets on top. You will have 6 stacks of 3 sheets each. Cut each stack in half crosswise so that you have 12 stacks.

7 Place equal portions of the banana mixture in the center at the short bottom edge of each stack of filo. Fold over the sides and roll into a cylinder.

8 Arrange the strudels on the prepared baking sheets. Bake for 12 minutes, or until golden brown.

9 Meanwhile, in a medium-sized bowl, whip the cream with the remaining 2 tablespoons granulated sugar.

10 Drain the raisins and fold into the whipped cream.

11 Place 2 strudels on each dessert plate. Sprinkle with confectioners' sugar. Place a spoonful of raisin brandy cream at the side, and serve immediately.

▶ **Filo dough is available in the freezer section of most supermarkets or specialty food stores.**

▶ **See page 41 for tip on handling filo dough.**

A WINTER DINNER

Potato Crêpes with Dried Tomatoes,
Goat Cheese, and Basil

Salmon with Onion Confit,
Winter Vegetables, and Red Wine Sauce

Pear Clafoutis

WINE SUGGESTIONS:

Sparkling Wine *(first course)*

Cabernet Sauvignon *(second course)*

Malvasia or German Auslese *(dessert)*

WHAT YOU CAN PREPARE AHEAD OF TIME

The day before: Prepare the tomato slices for the Potato Crêpes and allow to dry at room temperature. Cook and dice the beets and potatoes for the Salmon with Onion Confit. Dice the squash and turnip. Cover and refrigerate.

Early in the day: Make the Onion Confit for the Salmon with Onion Confit. Cover and refrigerate. Make the Red Wine Sauce for the Salmon with Onion Confit. Cover and refrigerate. Reheat just before serving.

Debra Ponzek's menu would be as appropriate at home after a day of winter sports as in an elegant dining room. Although Chef Ponzek is more than skilled at preparing sophisticated restaurant meals, she also has the rarer skill of rethinking her menus to make them accessible to the home cook. She realizes that the home menu needs to be much more practical and easy to execute with as much "do ahead" as possible. Debbie also has a special way of explaining her dishes, so that no one is ever intimidated by her suggestions. Needless to say, Debra Ponzek is one of the most popular De Gustibus chef/teachers.

◁ DEBRA PONZEK: Potato Crêpes with Dried Tomatoes, Goat Cheese, and Basil (recipe on page 64)

Potato Crêpes with Dried Tomatoes, Goat Cheese, and Basil

SERVES 6
PREPARATION TIME: ABOUT 35 MINUTES
COOKING TIME: ABOUT 30 MINUTES
DRYING TIME (TOMATOES ONLY): 8 TO 24 HOURS

This simple first course should only be made with very ripe tomatoes so that their flavor, when dried, is sweet, intense and a perfect balance for the potatoes and goat cheese. You can, if you choose, place the crêpes on top of a mesclun salad.

DRIED TOMATOES:

6 very ripe but firm plum tomatoes, cut into 1/8-inch thick slices
1/4 cup olive oil
2 tablespoons chopped fresh parsley
2 tablespoons chopped fresh thyme
2 tablespoons chopped fresh savory

POTATO CREPES:

3 large baking potatoes
2 tablespoons clarified butter (see page 12)
About 3 ounces fresh soft goat cheese, cut into 1/8-inch thick slices
Salt and freshly ground black pepper to taste
2 tablespoons chiffonade of fresh basil leaves

1 Assemble the *mise en place* trays for the dried tomatoes (see page 9). Line a baking sheet with parchment paper.

2 To prepare the tomatoes, place the slices on the prepared baking sheet. Sprinkle with a few drops of olive oil and the chopped herbs. Allow to dry at room temperature, uncovered, for at least 8 hours or up to 24 hours.

3 Assemble the *mise en place* trays for the rest of this recipe (see page 9).

4 To prepare the potato crêpes, peel the potatoes and cut, crosswise, into 1/16-inch thick slices or as thin as possible. Brush a nonstick skillet with about 1 teaspoon of the clarified butter, and place over medium heat. When the skillet is hot, lay 8 potato slices, slightly overlapping, to form a circle in the center of the skillet. Cook for 2 to 3 minutes, until golden brown on the bottom. Turn carefully with a wide spatula and cook for 2 to 3 minutes longer. Transfer to paper towels to drain. Cover with aluminum foil and keep warm. Continue making potato crêpes until you have 6.

5 Preheat the broiler.

6 Place a slice of goat cheese in the center of each crêpe. Cover the cheese with the dried tomatoes. Season with salt and pepper.

7 Place the crêpes on an ungreased baking sheet and broil for about 1 minute. Place on 6 warm serving plates, sprinkle with the basil chiffonade and drizzle with the remaining olive oil. Serve immediately.

▶ Peel and slice the potatoes just before making the crêpes, or they will discolor. Do not place the potatoes in water, or they will be too wet to crisp quickly.

▶ A mandoline or other vegetable slicer is the best tool for slicing the tomatoes and potatoes.

▶ If the weather is very humid, dry the tomatoes in a 200 degree F. oven for about 2 1/2 hours.

Salmon with Onion Confit, Winter Vegetables, and Red Wine Sauce

SERVES 6
PREPARATION TIME: ABOUT 1 HOUR AND 15 MINUTES
COOKING TIME: ABOUT 1 HOUR AND 45 MINUTES

This is a wonderfully aromatic dish, full of intense flavors that balance the delicate salmon. You could use almost any sweet, delicate fish, such as sea trout, white fish, or trout, as well as any combination of crisp vegetables you like.

RED WINE SAUCE:

2 tablespoons unsalted butter
1/3 cup chopped onions
1/3 cup chopped leeks
1/3 cup chopped celery
2 fresh thyme sprigs
1/2 pound salmon (or other fish) bones, well rinsed
1 1/2 cups red wine
1 cup Veal Stock (see page 13)
Salt and freshly ground black pepper to taste

WINTER VEGETABLES:

2 beets, scrubbed
5 small new potatoes, scrubbed
Salt and freshly ground black pepper to taste
1/2 large butternut squash, peeled, seeded, and cut into 1/4-inch dice
1 large turnip, peeled and cut into 1/4-inch dice
1 tablespoon unsalted butter
2 tablespoons chopped fresh parsley
2 tablespoons chopped fresh thyme

ONION CONFIT:

3 tablespoons duck fat or olive oil
3 pounds red onions, thinly sliced
5 tablespoons granulated sugar
3 tablespoons sherry vinegar
Salt and freshly ground black pepper to taste

SALMON:

2 teaspoons olive oil
6 six-ounce salmon fillets
Salt and freshly ground black pepper to taste

1 Assemble the *mise en place* trays for this recipe (see page 9).

2 To make the sauce, melt 2 tablespoons of the butter in a medium-sized saucepan over medium-high heat. Add the onion, leeks, celery, and thyme sprigs and stir to coat with the butter. Lay the fish bones on top of the vegetables, cover and reduce the heat to low. Cook for 5 to 10 minutes, or until any flesh remaining on the bones is opaque.

3 Stir in the wine and cook, uncovered, for about 15 minutes, or until the liquid is reduced by three-quarters. Add the stock and cook for about 30 minutes, or until the sauce is thick enough to coat the back of a spoon. Strain through a fine sieve into a small saucepan. Season to taste with salt and pepper. Set aside.

4 To prepare the winter vegetables, put the beets in a small saucepan and add enough water to cover. Bring to a boil over high heat. Reduce the heat and simmer for 20 minutes, or until tender when pierced with a fork. Drain and cool.

5 Meanwhile, put the potatoes in a medium-sized saucepan and add enough water to cover. Add a little salt to the water. Bring to a boil over high heat. Reduce the heat and simmer for about 12 minutes, or until tender when pierced with a fork. Drain and cool.

6 Peel the cooked beets and potatoes and cut into 1/4-inch dice. Toss with the squash and turnip, season with salt and pepper, and set aside.

7 To make the onion confit, melt the duck fat or oil in a large sauté pan over medium heat. Add the sliced red onions and sprinkle with the sugar. Cook, stirring occasionally, for 30 minutes, or until the onions are uniformly glazed and deep brown. Sprinkle with the vinegar and cook for 2 minutes more. Season to taste with salt and pepper. Remove from the heat and set aside.

8 Preheat the oven to 400 degrees F.

9 To prepare the salmon, in a large ovenproof sauté pan, heat the olive oil over medium-high heat. Season the salmon with salt and pepper and sear on both sides for 1

minute, or until just crisp. Transfer the pan to the oven and roast for 4 minutes, or until medium rare.

10 In a nonstick sauté pan, melt the butter over medium-high heat. Add the diced winter vegetables and season to taste with salt and pepper. Cook for 5 minutes, or until just crisp-tender and golden. Stir in the chopped herbs.

Remove from the heat and cover with aluminum foil to keep warm.

11 Meanwhile, heat the red wine sauce over low heat.

12 Place the onion confit on one side of 6 warm serving plates. Lay the salmon partially on the confit and spoon the vegetables on the other side of the salmon. Spoon the warm sauce around the vegetables and serve immediately.

Pear Clafoutis

Although a typically French dessert, usually made with cherries, clafoutis—here made with pears—is a welcome addition to the American table. Easy to prepare, it is delicious warm from the oven.

1 tablespoon unsalted butter, softened
1/2 cup plus 1 tablespoon granulated sugar
3 large eggs
1 vanilla bean split lengthwise or 2 teaspoons pure vanilla extract
1 1/2 cups heavy cream
1 tablespoon Poire William liqueur (pear liqueur)
6 tablespoons all-purpose flour, sifted
1 1/2 teaspoons ground cinnamon
4 ripe but firm Bartlett or Anjou pears

1 Preheat the oven to 375 degrees F. Assemble the *mise en place* trays for this recipe (see page 9). Butter an 11- by 7- by 2-inch rectangular or oval baking dish with 1 tablespoon of the butter. Sprinkle with 1 tablespoon of the sugar.

2 In a large bowl, beat the eggs and the remaining 1/2 cup of sugar until light yellow and fluffy.

3 Scrape the seeds from the vanilla bean into the eggs or add the extract. Beat in the cream and liqueur. Beat in the flour and cinnamon until well blended. Set aside while you prepare the pears.

4 Peel, quarter, core, and cut the pears lengthwise into 1/4-inch thick slices. Arrange the slices in the bottom of the prepared baking dish.

◁ DEBRA PONZEK: **Salmon with Onion Confit, Winter Vegetables, and Red Wine Sauce**

5 Pour the batter over the pears. Bake for 40 minutes, or until puffed up and firm. Remove from the oven and serve immediately, as the clafoutis will quickly deflate.

DEBRA PONZEK: **Pear Clafoutis**

A MODERN DINNER

Tuna Tartare and Herb Salad
Duck wth Turnips and Medjoul Dates
Warm Chocolate Cake

WINE SUGGESTIONS:

Sauvignon Blanc *(first course)*
Merlot or Côtes du Rhône *(second course)*
Late Bottled Vintage Port *(dessert)*

WHAT YOU CAN PREPARE AHEAD OF TIME

The day before: Prepare the sauce for the Duck with Turnips and Medjoul Dates. Cover and refrigerate. Reheat just before serving.

Early in the day: Make the vinaigrette for the Tuna Tartare and Herb Salad. Cover and refrigerate. Wash and dry the mesclun salad and fresh herbs for the Tuna Tartare and Herb Salad. Wrap in damp paper towels and refrigerate. Make the croutons for the Tuna Tartare and Herb Salad.

In the afternoon: Cook the turnips and dates for the Duck with Turnips and Medjoul Dates. Bake the Warm Chocolate Cake only about 3½ hours before serving. Cover and set aside at room temperature.

Alfred Portale is another favorite De Gustibus chef. He always impresses us with his stunning combinations of flavors, spectacular presentations, and clean, clear tastes.

Chef Portale's menu truly reflects his personality—a bit sardonic, wonderfully witty, and always congenial. His combination of flavors and robust American presentations leave our audiences awed. On top of all this, Alfred is a great teacher, very clear and precise—otherwise he would leave us all overwhelmed!

◁ ALFRED PORTALE: Tuna Tartare and Herb Salad (recipe on page 70)

Tuna Tartare and Herb Salad

The tuna must be absolutely pristine for this refreshing first course. Complex in presentation, it surprises by being quite easy to put together. However, it requires last-minute preparation and assembly.

GINGER VINAIGRETTE:

5 ounces fresh ginger, peeled
3/4 cup grapeseed oil, or more to taste
1/4 cup plus 2 tablespoons fresh lime juice, or more to taste
7 drops Tabasco
1 clove garlic, minced
1 shallot, minced

TUNA:

1 Japanese or hot-house cucumber, washed and dried
1 1/2 pounds sashimi-grade yellowfin tuna
2 scallions, trimmed and minced
Salt and freshly ground black pepper to taste

CROUTONS:

1 long, thin baguette
3 tablespoons extra-virgin olive oil

HERB SALAD:

2 cups mesclun salad, washed and dried
1/4 cup flat-leaf parsley leaves
1/4 cup inch-long chive stalks
2 tablespoons fresh mint leaves
2 tablespoons fresh cilantro leaves
2 tablespoons fresh chervil leaves

1 Preheat the oven to 375 degrees F. Assemble the *mise en place* trays for this recipe (see page 9).

2 To make the vinaigrette, grate the ginger. Wrap the grated ginger in a square of cheesecloth, hold it over a small bowl, and twist the cheesecloth tightly to extract the ginger juice. Stir in the grapeseed oil, lime juice, Tabasco, minced garlic, and shallot. Taste and adjust the flavors with additional oil or citrus juices, if necessary. Set aside.

3 Using the tines of a fork, make long, deep cuts down the length of the cucumber. Slice crosswise into very thin slices. Cover and refrigerate.

4 To prepare the tartare, cut the tuna into 1/4-inch dice. Place in a glass or ceramic bowl and add 3/4 cup of the Ginger Vinaigrette and the minced scallions and toss to mix. Season to taste with salt and pepper and set aside at room temperature.

5 To make the croutons, slice the baguette diagonally into 1/4-inch slices so that you have at least 18 slices. (Cut a few extra slices in case guests want more croutons.) Lay the bread slices on a baking sheet and bake for 5 minutes or until golden, turning once. Drizzle with the olive oil and set aside.

6 To make the salad, toss the salad and herbs in a bowl. Add the remaining Ginger Vinaigrette and toss to coat.

7 Place a 3-inch round ring mold or pastry cutter in the center of a chilled serving plate. Make a circle of overlapping cucumber slices around the outside circumference of the mold. Lightly pack one portion of the tuna mixture into the mold and lift off the mold. Stand 3 or 4 croutons around the tuna, leaning them slightly outward. Arrange about 1/2 cup of the herb salad on top of the tuna, in between the croutons. Working quickly, assemble the remaining plates. Serve immediately with extra croutons on the side.

▶ You can marinate the tuna in the vinaigrette for as long as 45 minutes ahead of time, but any longer will render the fish soft. Cover and refrigerate the fish during marinating, if making ahead.

▶ To replicate Chef Portale's presentation of this recipe exactly, put hoisin sauce in a squeeze bottle and dot each cucumber slice with a little sauce for extra garnish.

Duck with Turnips and Medjoul Dates

Ducks and dates are made for each other: both are wonderfully sweet and juicy. Although this recipe takes time to prepare because you must make Duck Stock, the actual preparation is surprisingly easy.

2 four-and-a-half-pound Muscovy ducks

SAUCE:

Reserved bones and trimmings from ducks
1 tablespoon olive oil
1 onion, coarsely chopped
3½ cups dry red wine
1 head garlic, halved crosswise
1 teaspoon black peppercorns
3 sprigs fresh thyme or ½ teaspoon dried thyme
2 bay leaves ,
½ teaspoon caraway seeds

DUCK:

6 tablespoons unsalted butter
4 large turnips, peeled and very thinly sliced
6 medjoul dates, pitted and thinly sliced lengthwise
4 teaspoons sweet butter
1 ounce olive oil
Salt and freshly ground black pepper

1 Preheat oven to 400 degrees F. Assemble the *mise en place* trays for the sauce portion of the recipe (see page 9).

2 Cut off the duck legs and cut apart at the joint. Remove the meat from thighs, leaving it intact; remove the breast halves from the carcass, leaving them intact. Cover and refrigerate the breast and thigh meat. Chop the duck bones and trimmings into pieces.

3 To make the sauce, spread the bones and trimmings in a single layer in a large roasting pan and roast, stirring several times, for about 20 minutes, or until lightly browned.

4 Meanwhile, heat the olive oil in a large sauté pan. Cook the onions over medium-high heat for about 10 minutes, until softened and lightly browned. Remove from the heat.

5 Transfer the bones to a large stockpot and add the onions. Add the wine and enough water to cover the bones. Add the garlic, peppercorns, thyme, bay leaves, and caraway seeds. Bring to a boil over high heat, and then reduce the heat and simmer, partially covered, for 4 to 6 hours, skimming any foam that rises to the surface during cooking. Add more water if necessary.

6 Spoon the fat from the surface of the stock, or blot it with a folded paper towel. Strain the stock through a sieve into a saucepan, pressing against the solids to extract as much liquid as possible. Discard the solids. Strain the stock a second time through a fine-mesh sieve into a saucepan. Bring to a boil over medium heat and cook for 20 to 30 minutes, until reduced to about 1½ cups. The sauce will be slightly syrupy. Set aside.

7 To prepare the duck, assemble the *mise en place* trays for the remaining ingredients (see page 9).

8 Melt 2 tablespoons of the butter in a large sauté pan over medium-high heat. Sauté the turnips for 3 to 4 minutes, until softened and lightly browned around the edges. Add the dates during the last minute of cooking and season to taste with salt and pepper, remove from the heat, and cover to keep warm.

9 Bring the duck sauce to a boil over high heat. Reduce to a simmer and whisk in the remaining 4 tablespoons of butter, a tablespoon at a time, waiting until each one is incorporated before adding the next. Adjust the seasonings and cover to keep warm.

10 In a large sauté pan, heat olive oil over medium heat. Season the duck breasts and thighs with salt and pepper and add to the pan, skin side down. Cook for 4 to 5 minutes, until the skin is crispy. Turn and cook for 4 to 5 minutes longer, until medium-rare. Transfer to a platter or cutting board and let rest for a few minutes.

11 Slice the breasts and thighs on the diagonal into thick slices. Fan the slices in a semi-circle around the center of 6 serving plates. Gather date slivers in a bunch, wrap them with a few turnip slices and stand them lengthwise in the center of each plate. Gently fold turnip slices to form rounded cushions and place around the bundle of dates so

that it stands up. Continue adding turnip folds to the base, and intersperse with more date slivers. Spoon the sauce around the outside of the duck, and in a circle around the base of the turnip mixture.

▶ **If serving six people and you don't want to plate the duck individually, fan the duck on a platter and create one turnip and date centerpiece, and serve the rest of the portions on the side.**

Warm Chocolate Cake

SERVES 6
PREPARATION TIME: ABOUT 30 MINUTES
BAKING TIME: ABOUT 1 HOUR
RESTING TIME: 2 HOURS

This is about the best chocolate cake you'll ever eat. You can serve it with whipped cream or, for even more indulgence, toasted almond ice cream.

1 pound semisweet chocolate, coarsely chopped
3 ounces bittersweet chocolate, coarsely chopped
1/2 cup plus 2 tablespoons strong brewed coffee
6 large eggs
1/2 cup plus 2 tablespoons granulated sugar
1 cup heavy cream
Whipped cream or ice cream, for serving (optional)

1 Preheat the oven to 325 degrees F. Assemble the *mise en place* trays for this recipe (see page 9). Butter a 10-inch round cake pan. Cut a 10-inch circle of parchment paper and fit it into the bottom of the pan. Lightly butter the parchment paper.

2 In the top half of a double boiler or in a heatproof bowl, combine the chocolates. Set over barely simmering water and allow to melt, stirring frequently. Remove from the heat, stir in the coffee, and mix until smooth. Set aside.

3 In the top half of a double boiler or in a heatproof bowl, combine the eggs and sugar. Set over boiling water and stir constantly until the sugar has dissolved and the mixture is warm. Reduce the heat to a gentle simmer.

4 Using a hand-held mixer set on medium speed, beat the egg mixture for about 5 minutes, or until it forms soft peaks. Remove the top half of the double boiler or the bowl from the heat. Gently fold a third of the beaten eggs into the melted chocolate. Fold in the rest of the egg mixture. Do not overmix; fold just until blended.

5 In a medium bowl, beat the cream until it forms stiff peaks. Gently fold into the chocolate mixture until well

blended. Scrape the batter into the prepared pan and smooth the top. Place the pan in a larger pan and add enough hot water to come 1/2 inch up the sides of the cake pan. Bake for 1 hour.

6 Turn off the oven and open the oven door for 1 minute. Close the door and allow the cake to rest in the oven for 2 hours.

7 Invert the cake onto a serving plate and lift off the pan. Peel off the parchment paper. Serve warm, with whipped cream or ice cream if desired.

ALFRED PORTALE: Warm Chocolate Cake

◁ ALFRED PORTALE: **Duck with Turnips and Medjoul Dates**

THE FLAVORS OF SPRING

Fresh Tuna with Maui Onions and Avocado

Grilled Salmon with Black Pepper and Ginger

Pecan Pie

WINE SUGGESTIONS:

Sparkling Wine *(first course)*

Sauvignon Blanc *(second course)*

Tawny Port *(dessert)*

WHAT YOU CAN PREPARE AHEAD OF TIME

Up to 1 week ahead: Make the pastry and line the tart pan for the Pecan Pie. Cover tightly and freeze.

Early in the day: Make the vinaigrette for the Fresh Tuna. Cover and refrigerate. Dice the onion for the Fresh Tuna. Cover and refrigerate. Make the sauce for the Grilled Salmon through step 3. Cover and refrigerate. Add the butter during reheating, just before serving. Fry the spinach leaves for the Grilled Salmon. Store, uncovered, in a dry place.

In the afternoon: Bake the pie. When cool, cover and set aside in a cool place.

Whenever Wolfgang Puck teaches at De Gustibus, we cannot keep the crowds from forming and there is always a waiting list of eager food enthusiasts. Not only is Chef Puck a magnet for our students, he also pulls remarkable flavors and tastes from the most simple ingredients.

Wolfgang is filled with good humor and his face is lit by a broad smile as he chops, minces, stirs, and mixes. He chats comfortably with his inquiring audience and makes it all seem effortless as he combines foods to bring out their maximum flavor. Never does one element overpower a dish. He and his food are absolutely joyful.

This menu is filled with the feelings of spring, much like Wolf himself. There is a slight Asian influence that adds a balance and intensity to the otherwise simple ingredients. Then he tops it off with a down-home American pie appropriate any time of year.

◁ WOLFGANG PUCK: Grilled Salmon with Black Pepper and Ginger (recipe on page 77)

Fresh Tuna with Maui Onions and Avocado

Simple yet sublime. Increase the portion sizes and you have a perfect summer's luncheon.

VINAIGRETTE:

Juice of 3 limes
1/4 cup plus 1 tablespoon soy sauce
1/3 cup extra-virgin olive oil
1 1/2 teaspoons minced fresh ginger
Freshly ground black pepper to taste

TUNA:

3/4 pound sashimi-grade yellowfin tuna, about 1 inch thick
3 cups radish sprouts, rinsed and dried
2 ripe avocados
1 cup diced Maui or other sweet onion
1 tablespoon golden caviar

1 Assemble the *mise en place* trays for this recipe (see page 9).

2 To make the vinaigrette, whisk together the lime juice, soy sauce, olive oil, and ginger in a glass or ceramic bowl. Season to taste with pepper. Set aside.

3 To prepare the tuna, slice the fish into 1/4-inch thick slices. Cut each slice into 3-inch triangles.

4 Place equal portions of the sprouts on one side of 6 chilled plates.

5 Peel, halve, and pit the avocados. Cut lengthwise into very thin slices. Fan an equal number of avocado slices around the other side of the plates from the sprouts. Arrange the tuna slices in the center of the plates. Sprinkle the onions on top of the tuna and place 1/2 teaspoon of caviar on top of the onions on each plate. Whisk the vinaigrette, and spoon over the tuna and avocado. Serve immediately.

WOLFGANG PUCK: Fresh Tuna with Maui Onions and Avocado

▶ Use ripe California avocados (black-skinned Haas) that give when held in the palm of the hand and pressed gently with your fingers. Underripe avocados will ripen at room temperature in a few days.

▶ Maui onions are sweet onions similar to Vidalia and Walla Walla. Any sweet onion works well in this recipe.

▶ Radish sprouts are easy to find, but you can substitute any sprout, or to maintain the peppery flavor use arugula or watercress greens.

Grilled Salmon with Black Pepper and Ginger

Exotic tastes simply presented make this a special entrée. It is easy to do on a grill, but equally good cooked under a hot broiler.

1½ cups white wine
¾ cup sherry
6 scallions, trimmed and chopped
5½ tablespoons chopped fresh ginger
½ cup heavy cream
8 tablespoons unsalted butter
Salt and freshly ground white pepper to taste
3 cups plus 3 tablespoons peanut oil
1 bunch spinach, trimmed, washed, and thoroughly dried
4½ tablespoons cracked black pepper
6 six-ounce fresh, skinless salmon fillets

1 Prepare a charcoal or gas grill or preheat the broiler. Assemble the *mise en place* trays for this recipe (see page 9).

2 In a medium-sized saucepan, combine the wine, sherry, scallions, and 1 tablespoon of the ginger. Bring to a simmer over medium heat and simmer for 10 to 12 minutes, or until reduced by half.

3 Slowly whisk in the cream and cook gently for 15 to 20 minutes, or until the sauce is thick enough to coat the back of a spoon.

4 Whisk the butter into the sauce, waiting until each tablespoon is incorporated before adding the next. Remove from the heat and season to taste with salt and white pepper. Strain through a fine sieve into a small saucepan. Set aside.

5 In a deep, heavy saucepan, heat 3 cups of the oil over medium-high heat. When very hot, cook the spinach leaves, a few at a time, for 20 seconds, or until crisp. Using a slotted spoon, remove the leaves from the oil and drain on paper towels.

6 Combine the remaining 4½ tablespoons ginger and the cracked pepper. Season the salmon with salt to taste, and then generously coat with the ginger-pepper mixture. Drizzle the remaining 3 tablespoons of oil over both sides

of the salmon. Grill or broil the salmon for 4 to 5 minutes on each side, or until firm but still rare in the center.

7 Meanwhile, in the top half of a double boiler, reheat the sauce over low heat.

8 Spoon the sauce into the center of 6 warm plates. Lay a salmon fillet on the sauce. Arrange the spinach leaves to the side, and serve immediately.

▶ Be sure the spinach leaves are completely dry before frying. If they are even a little wet, the oil will spatter. In any event, use caution when dropping them into the hot oil and do not crowd the pan. Although these can be fried ahead of time, they are best when fried immediately before serving.

Pecan Pie

Wolfgang's classic pecan pie is a perfect dessert to end this slightly Asian meal.

PIE PASTRY:

1¾ cups all-purpose flour, sifted
1 tablespoon granulated sugar
¼ teaspoon salt
12 tablespoons unsalted butter, cut into 1-inch pieces and chilled
2 large egg yolks
2 to 3 tablespoons heavy cream

FILLING:

1 cup light corn syrup
¾ cup packed light brown sugar
3 large eggs
2 large egg yolks
2 teaspoons pure vanilla extract
2 tablespoons unsalted butter
1½ cups pecan halves

■ Special Equipment: 10-inch fluted tart pan with removable bottom

1 Assemble the *mise en place* trays for this recipe (see page 9).

2 To make the pie pastry, in a food processor fitted with the metal blade, combine the flour, sugar, salt, and butter. Process until the mixture resembles fine meal.

3 Whisk together the egg yolks and 2 tablespoons cream. With the motor running, slowly add to the flour mixture and process until the dough comes together into a ball. Add additional cream if necessary to make a cohesive dough. Transfer the dough to a lightly floured surface. Pat into a circle about ½ inch thick. Wrap in plastic and refrigerate for 2 hours, or until well chilled.

4 Preheat the oven to 375 degrees F.

5 To make the filling, combine the corn syrup, brown sugar, eggs, egg yolks, and vanilla and whisk well.

6 Heat the butter in a small sauté pan over medium heat for 3 minutes, or until it is browned and gives off a nutty aroma. Immediately stir the butter into the corn syrup mixture.

7 On a lightly floured surface, roll out the dough to a 12-inch circle. Carefully fit it into a 10-inch fluted tart pan with removable bottom and trim off the excess. Set the tart pan in a baking sheet lined with foil.

8 Arrange the pecan halves in the bottom of the pastry shell. Carefully ladle the filling mixture over the pecans. Bake in the lower third of the oven for 40 to 45 minutes, or until a cake tester inserted into the center comes out clean. Transfer to a wire rack to cool to room temperature.

▶ The tart pan is set on a foil-lined baking sheet to catch any sugary overflow from the filling, so as to make cleanup easy.

◁ WOLFGANG PUCK: Pecan Pie

A MEAL FOR ALL SEASONS

Iced Sweet Pea Soup

*Quail with Coffee and Spice Rub
and White Bean Ragout*

Chocolate Bread Pudding

WINE SUGGESTIONS:

Sparkling Wine *(first course)*

Côtes du Rhône *(second course)*

Ruby Port *(dessert)*

WHAT YOU CAN PREPARE AHEAD OF TIME

Up to 1 week ahead: Prepare the Chicken Stock for the Iced Sweet Pea Soup (if making your own).

The day before: Make the Iced Sweet Pea Soup. Cover and refrigerate. Prepare the White Bean Ragout without adding the kale, parsley, and butter. Cover and refrigerate. Reheat, adding the remaining ingredients, just before serving. Prepare the spice rub for the Quail with Coffee and Spice Rub. Cover and store at cool room temperature.

Early in the day: Bake the Chocolate Bread Pudding. Cover with aluminum foil and reheat at 300 degrees F. for 15 minutes before serving.

A nne Rosenzweig has been teaching at De Gustibus almost as long as she has been Executive Chef at Arcadia, in New York City. According to Anne, De Gustibus was her first teaching experience, but she enjoyed it so much, and we thought her so good, she began to teach all over the country. Chef Rosenzweig loves to experiment with unusual ingredients and techniques. Although the coffee and spice rub for the quail in this menu seems bizarre, the taste is astonishingly delicious. In this dish, she has given us maximum flavor with a minimum of fat. Her dessert combines a traditional technique with contemporary flavor—something all dessert-lovers will appreciate.

◁ ANNE ROSENZWEIG: Iced Sweet Pea Soup (recipe on page 82)

Iced Sweet Pea Soup

Unusual flavors combine to make a wonderfully refreshing cold soup. However, when the weather requires a bit of warmth to start the meal, you can also serve it hot.

2 tablespoons coriander seeds
3 tablespoons unsalted butter
¾ cup minced Vidalia or other sweet onion
3½ cups Chicken Stock (see page 13)
5 cups fresh peas or thawed frozen petite peas
½ cup freshly grated coconut (see note)
1 cup heavy cream
1 cup tightly packed fresh spinach leaves
Salt and freshly ground white pepper to taste
2 to 3 tablespoons crème fraîche
¼ cup chopped fresh cilantro

1 Assemble the *mise en place* trays for this recipe (see page 9).

2 In a small sauté pan, toast the coriander seeds over medium heat for about 5 minutes, or until they begin to smoke and release their oils. Transfer to a plate to cool and then place in a spice grinder and process until fine.

3 In a large saucepan, melt the butter over medium heat. Add the onions, reduce the heat, and cook for 10 minutes, stirring occasionally, until the onions soften, but do not brown. Add the ground coriander and stock, increase the heat to medium, and cook for about 2 minutes, until heated through. Bring to a simmer and stir in the peas and coconut. Cook for about 5 minutes, or until the peas are tender. Stir in the cream and spinach and cook for about 1 minute, or until the spinach begins to wilt.

4 Transfer to a blender or a food processor fitted with the metal blade. Blend or process until smooth. Season to taste with salt and pepper. Pour into a glass or ceramic bowl and refrigerate for 4 hours, or until thoroughly chilled. Taste and adjust the seasoning.

5 Ladle the soup into 6 well-chilled, shallow soup bowls. Garnish each serving with a dollop of crème fraîche and a sprinkling of cilantro. Serve immediately.

▶ If you substitute packaged grated coconut for fresh, be sure to buy unsweetened coconut. If you prefer to grate fresh coconut, you may be able to buy a chunk of fresh coconut to grate, rather than having to purchase a whole coconut. Grate the coconut with a hand grater or grate in a food processor.

▶ You can substitute sour cream for the crème fraîche. Crème fraîche is available in the refrigerated food section of specialty stores and some supermarkets.

ANNE ROSENZWEIG: Iced Sweet Pea Soup

Quail with Coffee and Spice Rub and White Bean Ragout

SERVES 6
PREPARATION TIME: ABOUT 45 MINUTES
COOKING TIME: ABOUT 1 HOUR AND 30 MINUTES
MARINATING TIME: 8 HOURS

This is an unusual, taste bud-shocking combination, yet absolutely delicious. The mellow bean ragout offers the perfect complement to the quail.

SPICE RUB:

2 tablespoons sesame seeds
25 coriander seeds
20 black peppercorns
3 cloves
2 juniper berries
1/4-inch piece cinnamon stick
1/2-inch piece bay leaf
3 tablespoons espresso coffee beans
1 teaspoon salt, or more, to taste

QUAIL:

12 quail, butterflied
3 ounces slab bacon, cut in 1/4-inch dice
1 cup finely chopped carrots
1 cup finely chopped onions
1 cup Chicken Stock (see page 13)
1/4 cup red wine
5 1/2 cups cooked Great Northern beans (see page 15) or rinsed and drained canned white beans
1 tablespoon minced fresh thyme
4 cups chopped fresh kale
1/2 cup chopped fresh parsley
4 tablespoons unsalted butter
Freshly ground black pepper to taste
2 tablespoons corn oil

1 Preheat the oven to 300 degrees F. Assemble the *mise en place* trays for this recipe (see page 9).

2 Put the sesame and coriander seeds, peppercorns, cloves, juniper berries, cinnamon stick, and bay leaf in separate, flattened piles on a non-stick baking sheet with sides. Toast in the oven for 25 to 30 minutes, or until the sesame seeds are golden brown. Remove from the oven and let cool slightly.

3 Measure 1 tablespoon of the sesame seeds and set aside. Place the remaining seeds and spices in a spice grinder. Add the coffee beans and 1 teaspoon salt. Process until finely ground.

4 Rub the spice mixture evenly over the skin side of the quail. Cover and refrigerate for 8 hours or overnight.

5 Preheat the oven to 325 degrees F.

6 In a large saucepan, sauté the bacon over medium heat for about 5 minutes, or until all the fat has been rendered. Add the carrots and onions and sauté for 3 minutes. Add the stock and wine and bring to a simmer. Cook, stirring occasionally, for 15 to 20 minutes, or until most of the liquid has evaporated. Stir in the beans and thyme. Cook for about 4 minutes. Stir in the kale, parsley, and butter. Season to taste with salt and pepper. Remove from the heat and keep warm.

7 In a large, heavy skillet, heat the oil over medium-high heat. Add 3 or 4 quail, skin-side down, and cook for about 2 minutes, or until lightly browned. Turn and cook for 4 to 6 minutes longer, or until medium rare. Sprinkle with some of the reserved sesame seeds and remove from the pan. Cover and keep warm in the oven. Cook the remaining quail.

8 Spoon the ragout onto 6 warm plates. Lay 2 quail on either side of the plate and serve immediately.

▶ Ask the butcher to butterfly the quail. This entails splitting the birds open along the backbone, removing the backbone, and gently beating the sides of the quail with a cleaver to flatten slightly. If quail are unavailable, substitute 1-pound Rock Cornish game hens and serve one per person. Prepared quail are available through mail-order sources (see Sources, page 93).

▶ You can substitute Swiss chard for the kale.

▶ If you don't want to use bacon to flavor the beans, use an equal amount of smoked turkey leg.

Chocolate Bread Pudding

Here is a simply delicious version of an old-fashioned dessert.

12 one-inch-thick slices brioche (or other richly flavored egg bread such as challah)
¾ cup unsalted butter, melted
8 ounces bittersweet chocolate, coarsely chopped
3 cups heavy cream
1 cup milk
1 cup granulated sugar
12 large egg yolks
1 teaspoon pure vanilla extract
⅛ teaspoon salt
1 cup heavy cream, softly whipped (optional)

1 Preheat the oven to 425 degrees F. Assemble the *mise en place* trays for this recipe (see page 9).

2 Brush both sides of the bread slices with the melted butter. Place on a baking sheet and toast in the oven for 7 to 10 minutes, or until golden brown. Set aside.

3 Place the chocolate in a medium-sized bowl set over a saucepan of very hot, not simmering, water. The bottom of the bowl should not touch the water. Stir frequently until melted.

4 In a medium-sized saucepan, heat the cream and milk for about 5 minutes, over medium heat to just under a boil. Do not boil. Remove from the heat.

5 In a large bowl, whisk together the sugar and egg yolks until well blended. Gradually whisk the hot cream and milk mixture. Strain through a fine sieve into a bowl and skim off any foam.

6 Whisk the melted chocolate into the yolk mixture. Stir in the vanilla and salt.

7 Arrange the toasted bread in 2 overlapping rows in a 9-by 13-inch baking pan. Pour the chocolate mixture over the bread. Cover with plastic wrap and place a smaller baking pan on top of the bread so that the slices stay sub-

merged. Add weights if necessary. Refrigerate for 1 hour or until the bread is soaked through.

8 Preheat the oven to 325 degrees F.

9 Remove the smaller pan and plastic wrap from the bread pudding. Cover with aluminum foil and punch a few holes in the top to allow the steam to escape. Place in a larger pan and pour in enough water to come ½ inch up the sides of the smaller pan. Bake for about 1 hour and 45 minutes, or until all the liquid has been absorbed and the pudding has a glossy look.

10 Cut the pudding into squares and serve warm with whipped cream, if desired.

ANNE ROSENZWEIG: **Chocolate Bread Pudding**

◁ ANNE ROSENZWEIG: **Quail with Coffee and Spice Rub and White Bean Ragout (recipe on page 83)**

A PASTA PARTY

Smoked Salmon, Salmon Roe, and Pasta Salad

Fusilli with Tomatoes and Bread Crumbs

Apricot and Cherry Tart

WINE SUGGESTIONS:

Sparkling Wine *(first course)*

Pinot Grigio or Sauvignon Blanc *(second course)*

Late Harvest Muscat or Riesling *(dessert)*

WHAT YOU CAN PREPARE AHEAD OF TIME

Early in the day: Prepare all the components for the Smoked Salmon, Salmon Roe, and Pasta Salad. Cover and refrigerate. Prepare the bread crumbs for the Fusilli with Tomatoes and Bread Crumbs. Cover and store at room temperature. Prepare the tomato and herb mixture for the Fusilli. Cover and store at room temperature.

Up to 4 hours ahead: Make the Apricot and Cherry Tart. Cover and set aside in a cool place.

For one of her very rare De Gustibus appearances, Alice Waters spent three days giving classes. Before her arrival, she sent boxes of the most beautiful fruits, vegetables, and herbs from the Chinos Farm in San Diego, California. The colors, textures, and aromas transported us to the sensual Mediterranean.

The influence of the California farmers on Alice most certainly shows in her cooking. With these marvelous ingredients, she created a tempting summer pasta buffet, with only the fusilli requiring last-minute preparation. This was a class that we all remember with all of our senses.

◁ ALICE WATERS: Apricot and Cherry Tart (recipe on page 91)

Smoked Salmon, Salmon Roe, and Pasta Salad

SERVES 6
PREPARATION TIME: ABOUT 30 MINUTES
COOKING TIME: ABOUT 25 MINUTES
CHILLING TIME: ABOUT 4 HOURS

This salad will never seem as delicious to us as it was the first time Alice made it. But, if you use only the best ingredients, you'll come very close!

Juice of 2 limes (about 1/3 cup)
2 teaspoons Dijon mustard
Grated zest of 1 lemon
12 quail eggs (see note)
Salt and freshly ground black pepper to taste
1/2 cup extra-virgin olive oil, or to taste
2/3 pound thin green beans or haricot verts, trimmed
1 bunch fresh cilantro, washed and dried
1 bunch watercress, washed and dried
1 pound dried tubular pasta such as ditali or penne, or small shells
1/2 cup chopped pitted Niçoise olives
1 1/2 cups tiny fresh peas
5 scallions, trimmed and sliced
8 ounces thinly sliced smoked salmon, cut into narrow strips
6 ounces salmon caviar

1 Assemble the *mise en place* trays for this recipe (see page 9).

2 In a glass or ceramic bowl, whisk together the lime juice, mustard, and lemon zest. Set aside.

3 Put the quail eggs in a medium-sized saucepan and add enough cold water to cover. Bring to a boil over high heat. Immediately remove from the heat, drain, and rinse under cold running water.

4 Peel the quail eggs and slice in half lengthwise. Arrange on a plate and season to taste with salt, pepper, and 2 tablespoons of the olive oil. Cover and refrigerate.

5 In a medium-sized saucepan of boiling salted water, blanch the beans for 2 minutes, or until bright green and crisp-tender. Drain and refresh under cold running water. Pat dry and set aside.

6 Remove the leaves from half of the cilantro and watercress and chop the leaves. Set these aside. Trim the remaining cilantro and watercress sprigs, wrap in damp paper towels, and refrigerate.

7 In a large pot, bring 4 quarts of salted water to a boil over high heat. Cook the pasta until *al dente*. Drain well.

8 Transfer the pasta to a large serving bowl, add the remaining 6 tablespoons of olive oil and toss well. Stir in the lime dressing, chopped cilantro and watercress, beans, olives, peas, and scallions until well mixed. Stir in the salmon and caviar. Wipe the edge of the bowl. Cover and refrigerate for 4 hours, or until well chilled.

9 When ready to serve, garnish the salad with the reserved cilantro and watercress sprigs, and nestle the quail eggs among them. Serve immediately.

▶ Quail eggs are sold in specialty stores. Hens' eggs are too large to substitute. If you cannot find quail eggs, omit them from the recipe.

▷ ALICE WATERS: Smoked Salmon, Salmon Roe, and Pasta Salad

Fusilli with Tomatoes and Bread Crumbs

SERVES 6
PREPARATION TIME: ABOUT 25 MINUTES
COOKING TIME: ABOUT 1 HOUR AND 25 MINUTES (1 HOUR FOR THE BREAD CRUMBS)

You must have very ripe, sweet tomatoes and good rustic bread for the true taste to come through in this simple but delicious dish.

1 large loaf country-style bread, crust removed
1/2 cup extra-virgin olive oil
4 cloves garlic, chopped
12 large, ripe, red tomatoes, cored, peeled, seeded, and chopped
1 large bunch fresh parsley, chopped
1/2 cup fresh basil leaves, chopped
6 sprigs fresh thyme leaves, chopped
Salt and freshly ground black pepper to taste
Balsamic or red wine vinegar to taste (optional)
1 1/2 pounds dried fusilli pasta

1 Preheat the oven to 275 degrees F. Assemble the *mise en place* trays for this recipe (see page 9).

2 Cut the bread into pieces. In a food processor fitted with the metal blade, process the bread, in batches, to coarse crumbs. You will have about 6 cups of crumbs. Spread in a shallow baking tray and toast in the oven for 1 hour, or until dry and crisp but not brown.

3 In a large sauté pan, heat the olive oil over medium heat. Add the bread crumbs and garlic and cook, stirring constantly, for 10 minutes, or until the crumbs are golden. Pour into a bowl and set aside.

4 In a glass or ceramic bowl, combine the tomatoes and chopped herbs. Season to taste with salt and pepper. Add a splash of vinegar to intensify the flavor of the tomatoes, if you desire.

5 In a large pot, bring 4 quarts of salted water to a boil over high heat. Cook the pasta until *al dente*. Drain well.

6 Transfer the pasta to a warm, shallow serving bowl. Pour the tomatoes over the top and toss to combine. Add the bread crumbs and toss to combine. Serve immediately.

▶ **This is a dish that waits for no one. Serve it as soon as it is assembled, or the bread crumbs will turn soggy.**

Alice Waters: Fusilli with Tomatoes and Bread Crumbs

Apricot and Cherry Tart

The fruit must be absolutely fresh and perfectly ripe to make this tart. Of course you could substitute other deliciously ripe fruit.

1 ten-inch sheet frozen puff pastry, partially thawed
1/2 cup crushed amaretti (Italian macaroons)
1 large egg yolk beaten with 2 teaspoons heavy cream, for egg wash
1 1/2 pounds Bing cherries, pitted
1 pound ripe apricots, halved and pitted
1 to 2 tablespoons sugar
3 tablespoons apricot jam
1 teaspoon Kirschwasser, or other eau de vie
Vanilla ice cream, for serving (optional)

1 Preheat the oven to 400 degrees F. Place a baking stone in the bottom of the oven and let it heat for at least 30 minutes. Assemble the *mise en place* trays for this recipe (see page 9).

2 On a lightly floured work surface, roll out the puff pastry between 2 sheets of wax paper to a circle about 14 inches in diameter. Carefully fit into a 10-inch fluted tart pan with a removable bottom, and trim the excess pastry. Freeze the tart shell for 30 minutes.

3 Sprinkle the bottom of the tart shell with the amaretti. Using a pastry brush, generously coat the edges of the pastry with the egg wash.

4 Arrange a circle of cherries around the outer edge of the tart, pressing them together as tightly as possible. Arrange a circle of apricot halves, pitted side down, inside the circle of cherries, pressing together as tightly as possible. Continue making circles until the tart is filled. Fill in any holes with remaining cherries and make sure the fruit is tightly packed into the shell. Sprinkle the top with sugar to taste.

5 Bake for 30 minutes, in the bottom third of the oven, until the pastry is golden and the fruit is tender. Transfer to a wire rack to cool slightly.

6 Meanwhile, in a small saucepan, melt apricot jam with the Kirschwasser over low heat. When softened, brush over the top of the warm tart. Cut into wedges and serve warm, with ice cream if desired.

▶ **Baking stones, which can be bought in kitchen shops and houseware stores, intensify the oven heat and help cook the bottom of tarts, breads, pizzas, and other baked goods. Although you can make this recipe without one, the tart may be slightly soft in the middle.**

▶ **You can also use unglazed ceramic tiles, also found in most cookware stores, to line the botom of the oven.**

Glossary

Aïoli: A pungent, garlic-flavored mayonnaise commonly used in the Provence region of France.

Al dente: An Italian term meaning, literally, "to the tooth." Most often used to describe pasta that has been cooked until it is just tender but still offers some resistance to the tooth when chewed. Can also be used to describe the degree to which certain vegetables should be cooked.

***Bâton* (or *bâtonnet*):** The shape of a vegetable that has been trimmed into a small, thin stick.

Bok choy: A mild-flavored Chinese cabbage with creamy white stalks and soft green leaves that rather resemble fat celery in shape. Also known as Chinese mustard cabbage. Napa cabbage can be used as a substitute.

Bouquet garni: A mixture of herbs and/or spices tied in a cheesecloth bag. Used to flavor soups, stews, stocks, and sauces.

Chiffonade: A preparation of greens, classically sorrel, chicory, or lettuce, cut into strips of varying degrees of thickness. Easily done by rolling the leaves up cigar fashion and slicing crosswise. Used as a garnish for soups and cold hors d'oeuvres.

Chile paste: A strongly seasoned Asian condiment made from fermented beans, chile peppers, and, often, garlic.

Cilantro: Pungent herb that looks like flat-leaf parsley, used to flavor Asian, Indian, and Latin American dishes. The bright green leaves are sometimes referred to as Chinese parsley or fresh coriander. Cilantro is widely available. There is no substitute: do not use coriander seeds instead!

Clarified butter: Butter that has been heated and skimmed so that all of the milk solids are removed, leaving only the clear, yellow fat. See page 12 for instructions for clarifying butter.

Coriander seeds: Yellow-tan seeds with a taste somewhat like an herb-scented lemon. Used in Asian cooking, pickling, and in some baked goods. Coriander seed cannot be used in place of fresh coriander or cilantro.

Crème fraîche: In France, thickened, unpasteurized cream; in America, pasteurized cream thickened with added fermenting agents. Tastes rather like slightly sweet sour cream.

Eau de vie: Literally, "water of life" in French, the term refers to a clear, potent spirit distilled from fermented fruit juice.

Fava beans: Pale, tannish-green, flat beans with a tough outer skin that must be removed, usually by blanching, before eating. Used frequently in Mediterranean and Middle Eastern cuisine.

Filo (also phyllo): Tissue paper-thin Greek pastry dough, usually prepared by stacking buttered layers which enclose sweet or savory mixtures. Available fresh or frozen in most supermarkets.

Frisée: A tangy, curly-leafed endive relative, often called curly endive. Its pale green leaves are used in salads.

Grapeseed oil: Light, almost flavorless oil extracted from grape seeds. Excellent for cooking as it has a high smoking point.

Great northern white beans: Creamy white dried haricot beans, slightly kidney-shaped, that have a mellow, sweet taste when cooked.

Hoisin sauce: Sweet, slightly spicy Chinese condiment made from soy beans, chile peppers, garlic, and spices. Deep red in color, it is used as an accent for all types of dishes. Available canned or bottled in Asian markets, specialty food stores, and many supermarkets.

Kirschwasser: Clear brandy distilled from cherry juice and pits.

Le Puy lentils: Dusky green, dried French lentils with the seed coat intact.

Mandoline: A stainless steel vegetable slicer composed of a folding stand and two blades. Used to cut vegetables into uniform slices or matchsticks.

Maui onions: Sweet, mild, crisp onions grown on Maui in the Hawaiian Islands, in season from April through July. Vidalia and Walla Walla onions can be substituted for Maui onions.

Mesclun: In France, a mixture of very young shoots and leaves of wild plants used for salads. Now commercially available in the United States, mesclun can also contain baby lettuces and leafy herbs.

Muscovy duck: Domestically raised duck, gamier in flavor than most, almost always served rare as it has a tendency to dry out when cooked.

Nori: Very thin sheets of dried seaweed, ranging from dark green through deep violet to black, generally used to enclose sushi or rice balls, or as a garnish. Available in Asian and specialty markets either toasted or untoasted.

Pesto: A Genoan raw sauce traditionally made by grinding herbs in a mortar and pestle. Today, classic pesto is made with fresh basil, garlic, pine nuts, grated Parmesan cheese, and olive oil. Contemporary variations are made from parsley and cilantro, with other nuts and cheeses. Mainly used as a pasta sauce, but may be used to flavor many other dishes, too.

Phyllo: See filo.

Poire William: A clear *eau de vie* made from pears. Often sold with a whole pear inside the bottle.

Provençal: Used to identify food prepared in the style of the dishes of southeastern France, usually incorporating tomatoes, garlic, and olive oil and often anchovies, eggplant, and/or olives as well.

Quince: A large, yellow fall fruit with dry, astringent flesh that tastes like a cross between a pear and an apple. It is always eaten cooked.

Ragout: A thick, highly seasoned stew.

Render: To melt animal fat over very low heat to separate the liquid fat from any meat, skin or tissue particles. Usually, the fat is then strained for clarity.

Roux: A cooked mixture of fat and flour used to thicken sauces or soups. White and blond *roux* are made from butter. Brown *roux* is usually made with meat pan drippings.

Sachet: See *Bouquet garni*

Sashimi-grade tuna: Tuna of the freshest, highest quality, which can be used for sashimi—Japanese sliced raw fish.

Sear: To brown meat or poultry by cooking over (or under) intense heat. This process is used to seal in the juices before longer cooking.

Shiitake mushrooms: Cultivated, full-flavored, dark brown "wild" mushrooms with broad caps ranging from 3 to 10 inches in diameter. Widely available both fresh and dried.

Soba noodles: Japanese noodles made from buckwheat flour. Available in Asian markets and many supermarkets.

Tahini: A thick paste made from ground sesame seeds. Used in Middle Eastern cooking.

Tartare: Coarsely chopped raw meat or fish, seasoned with herbs, salt, and pepper and eaten uncooked.

Truss: To hold meat or poultry in a compact shape by sewing it together with a trussing needle threaded with kitchen twine, or by tying the meat or poultry with kitchen twine.

Wonton wrappers: Paper-thin dough squares or rounds used in Chinese cooking to enclose savory fillings. These dumplings are then boiled, steamed, or fried. Available in Asian markets, specialty food stores, and some supermarkets.

Yellowfin tuna: A large tuna with pale pink flesh. Often used raw for sushi, sashimi, and tartare.

Sources for Spices and other Ingredients

Quail, other game birds, smoked products

Nodine's Smokehouse, Inc.
P.O. Box 1787
Torrington, CT 06790
1-800-222-2059

D'Artagnan
399–419 St. Paul Ave.
Jersey City, NJ 07306
(800) 327-8246
(201) 792-0748

Japanese ingredients

Katagiri & Company, Inc.
224 East 59th Street
New York, NY 10022
(212) 755-3566

Chinese ingredients

Kam Man
200 Canal Street
New York, NY 10013
(212) 571-0330

Spices

Penzey's Spice House Ltd.
P.O. Box 448
Waukesha, WI 53187
(414) 574-0277
Mail order catalog available

Kalustyan Orient Export Trading Corp.
123 Lexington Ave.
New York, NY 10016
(212) 685-3451

Index

CONVERSION CHART

WEIGHTS AND MEASURES

1 teaspoon = 5 milliliters

1 tablespoon = 3 teaspoons = 15 milliliters

1/8 cup = 2 tablespoons = 1 fluid ounce = 30 milliliters

1/4 cup = 4 tablespoons = 2 fluid ounces = 59 milliliters

1/2 cup = 8 tablespoons = 4 fluid ounces = 118 milliliters

1 cup = 16 tablespoons = 8 fluid ounces = 237 milliliters

1 pint = 2 cups = 16 fluid ounces = 473 milliliters

1 quart = 4 cups = 32 fluid ounces = 946 milliliters (.946 liter)

1 gallon = 4 quarts = 16 cups = 128 fluid ounces = 3.78 liters

1 ounce = 28 grams

1/4 pound = 4 ounces = 114 grams

1 pound = 16 ounces = 454 grams

2.2 pounds = 1,000 grams = 1 kilogram